"LOUISE BUTTERSKY"

Written by

TONY ANDREWS

Illustrations by

Mark Elmer

ISBN :

WWW.TONYANDREWSMUSIC.COM

Message from Tony Andrews,

Hi-ya, I have something important to say...

"GO AFTER YOUR DREAM!"

It doesn't matter what age you are, you might be thirteen, you may be ninety-five. I simply want to remind you, and encourage you to

GO FOR IT!

It seems that a lot of people 'just get by,' with a lack of happiness in their hearts. Well, in my opinion, I think that sucks! Unhappy people are not really living. So please dig down deep into your soul. Dare to step away from your comfort zone. Find what makes you passionate, find what makes you happy, seek the thing that sets your heart on fire, and be bold enough to

GIVE IT EVERYTHING YOU'VE GOT!

Dear Reader,

I hope you enjoy this roller-coaster story, I wrote it for you, all in the name of fun. Louise has so much to tell you.

I would like to wish you a long happy life, filled with good friends, great inner peace, and a little bit of laughter every day.

Love from Tony and Billy-boy x

Photo by Amanda Coplans

Tony Andrews is a tall English author and singer-songwriter. He was born in Finsbury Park, North London, and he loves going to the beach with his dog (Billy).

Meet The Gang

**It's crazy times for Louise, when a
Laundrette Lady takes her into another world,
where many dangerous events
and eccentric characters await her.
In this world, a whiskey-drinking witch
has very dark plans for this innocent little girl.
Join Louise in her adventures, and see how
TEAMWORK MAKES THE DREAMWORK!**

Invitation for you...

Let your wild imagination swim and dance

with mine, we can share a few laughs, as we

giggle, grow and shine.

The time has come for you to jump into

the fun fantasy world of

'LOUISE BUTTERSKY.'

I hope you enjoy this eccentric adventure,

I truly want my readers to be happy,

so just before you begin this book,

Please visit Youtube, and play a

Fun, Silly Song Called...

"BAMBOO"

(THE HAPPIEST SONG IN THE WORLD)

CHAPTERS

CHAPTER 1

HI, MY NAME IS LOUISE

I'm a true-blue weirdo, ha-ha. Hey, how's it going? Louise Buttersky here. Would it be okay if I shared my story with you? Lots of strange things have happened to me in my life, beautiful things, magical things, things that changed me deep inside forever, made me stronger. I've been on some wild adventures, and I must say, I've had my fair share of crazy moments. I really would like to tell you everything about me, I won't leave a single thing out, I promise. Let me start by sharing my very first memory with you: I was three and a half years old, sitting in the back seat of Dad's car, gazing out the front windscreen. Quickly parking in a bus stop, both my folks rushed off to buy some groceries, well, that's what they said, but when they returned they both hopped back in the car with four bulging heavy bin liners, they chucked them in the back seat with me. I remember how jumpy they were, my folks were acting so funny, celebrating like they'd just won first prize on a TV game show, something spooky was going on here all right. Dad quickly started the car and sped off down the street. Well, kiss my sweet rosy cheeks, my wild parents had just robbed a bank! My Pops was laughing his heads off. I was way too young to fully understand all this, all I remember was a strong feeling of happiness and wild excitement in the car, their adrenaline was pumped to the MAX! This was great energy to be exposed to, I found myself smiling and laughing along with them.

Dad drove a very old car; it was a red 1975 Volkswagen Beetle. In some countries they call that car a 'Bug' – ours was rusty and shabby, the old engine sounded like an old vintage John Deere 'sit-on' lawnmower, I loved that car so much, it was a great little runner, beetles are honest, fun and cheap to run, we called ours 'Sean.' It sounds silly to say this but I was emotionally attached to Sean. That rusty old banger was part of the family.

We got away with the bank job. Dad's plan worked like a sweet dream; a huge convoy of old VW Beetles drove through London that morning, they were on their way to a Bug-Jam car show, down in Brighton, a groovy summer time Beetle gathering, so we just tagged along with them. There were over a thousand Beetles on the motorway that day, it was so cool, this made it super-easy for us to blend-in and hide from the cops, ha-ha, nice move Dad.

Now, a pretty bizarre thing happened to me on the way down to Brighton, it was a little bit freaky but very fantastic. A small red-chested robin, wearing a tiny aviators hat, flew alongside our car as we bombed it down the highway; he kept us company on the M23. I remember this vividly, like it was yesterday. The robin kept looking and winking at me through the window. After tipping his tiny hat several times, he began to wave at me with his little wing. Gee-Whiz! He looked so funny. This cheeky enthusiastic little guy gave me the giggles for ten minutes. "What's so funny, Louise?" Asked my Mum. I immediately pointed at the little rascal, but every time she turned to have a look, he ducked down and flew out of sight; he was a crafty old bugger. Now, for a long time I thought that robin was just a crazy character in my imagination, but it turns out I really did see him, he is now one of my friends; I will tell you more about him later. Arriving in Brighton, we checked-in to The Grand Hotel, located right on the sea-front. It's a wham-bam-killer-posh-place, very classy and uppity. There were two marvellous Greek marble statues standing guard, out by the main entrance, Socrates and Plato, they pondered over the spinning doors. And the very first thing you see when you walk in, is a huge black majestic shiny grand piano, it was sick. We stayed there for two sunny weeks, it was a great place to hide-out, the tip-top-weather was flip-flop-tastic!

I remember the morning Dad treated me to a nice little watch from the hotel gift shop, it has a tiny little shooting star on its face. I love it so much! I still have it today, but it's all worn out now. I'll always remember what Dad said when he presented it to me. "Never forget who you are, my little sweetheart. You're a perfect magnificent shooting star!" When placing the petite watch on my little wrist Dad stole a quick kiss from me, then he picked me up and tickled me senseless, till I cried out with laughter. My Pops always knew how to make me smile. He's dead now. Ha-ha, just kidding. Before heading back to London, my folks decided to buy a new car, we ended up purchasing a small 1969 British-racing-green Mini Cooper. Poor old Sean had to go; he was too much of a connection to the bank job now. I know this sounds crazy, but I cried when we said goodbye to that rusty old bucket. When I'm older, I'm gonna buy a beetle for myself, a nice top-less yellow one, that's my favourite colour. Heading back to London in our new mini was a snug ride, my safety chair was squashed in the back seat, between two large red suitcases. I was blissfully happy because I had Lemon on my lap (he's my favourite teddy,) and my new watch on my wrist. I had absolutely no idea how to tell the time; I just loved looking at the shooting star on its face. Mum and Dad were blissfully happy too, because both suitcases were completely filled with cash!

We were filthy rich my love! Groovy baby! And...as a little bonus, I saw that crazy-fruit-loop robin again, on the exact same stretch of the M23 motorway, just as we drove past Gatwick airport. About a month after the robbery Dad decided to buy a nice little cottage in Devon, he picked a small quiet town by the seaside. Dad wanted to get far away from London, the busy city vibes were putting too much stress on his heart, he wanted a slower pace of life, and he swears to God that fish and chips taste nicer by the seaside. It's true, they do. So off we went to Devon; it was like going on a holiday that we never came back from, happy days! Our new cottage was tiny, but the back garden was massive, the neglected black and white patio looked like an old giant chessboard, lot of dandelions growing through the cracks, they grew everywhere. On the back lawn there must have been over a thousand daisies, and at least a hundred daffodils towering over them, and right at the very back, by the fence, stood a gigantic oak tree, with its very own rustic treehouse. This was a great place for me to paint, draw and read, in the summer months. We were just two streets away from the beach. I could jump out of bed in the morning and have my feet in the sand in less than five minutes, sometimes I dashed off for a brave dip in the ocean with Dad, and yes it was freezing cold, but only for the first two minutes. It's a great way to start the day, if you're nutty and tenacious.

My eccentric cockney London Dad really got into his fish and chips, so much so that after living in Devon for a few months, he decided to open up his own fish and chips restaurant, right on the seafront; he became a fish and chip-ologist, and just a few months later, he decided to get a swimming pool dug out in the backyard, this was great at first, but half a year down the line he started using it as a storage tank, for all his fish, which is a bit 'waco' if you ask me. He's a bit of an odd-ball my old man. He loves a good swim, and so does Mum, but she refuses to use the pool now, it's too stinky! Dad still swims in it, with or without fish, crazy fool! Now, back when I was just shy of six years old, I had a kooky life-changing accident in that pool. My cousin Richie accidentally pushed me in, way over in the deep end. Fortunately, there were no fish in it at the time. This all happened on a cold December morning, right in the middle of a snowball fight. Richie-boy had a cheeky devious plan, his aim was to hold me down in a headlock and stuff a freezing cold snowball down the back of my coat, nice hey. He ran at me like a wild bull, but the dumb twit didn't slow down in time. Sliding on the frosty grass, Richie bashed into me like a big bowling ball whacking down the last standing pin. I flew up into the air like a lightweight barbie doll, and crash-landed 'head-first' into the freezing cold pool. Holy smoking flap-jacks! This was an awfully intense trip, the shock was totally electrifying!

As I smashed through the ice, it felt like I was being stabbed by a million pins and needles - sweet jumping jelly beans! I know Richie didn't mean to push me in, he swore it was an accident, he's such a dopey salami-head. Close your eyes and try to imagine yourself standing at the top of Mount Everest, in a pink bikini. Or picture yourself sleeping in a meat freezer when you're butt-naked. Well, that's how cold I felt in that pool. My body went into a state of complete shock, I slipped into a trance, as I sank like an anvil. I think my heart stopped beating for a while. I was down there for an hour and a half, I guess I died. Richie lives in Wales now, but just the other day we had a telephone conversation all about the 'swimming pool accident,' and this is what old Richie-boy said: "Louise, I remember everything. I was looking at you in the water, and you were long gone. I waited and waited for you to pop your head back up, but you didn't move at all, you just sat there at the bottom of that ice cold pool like a boxer who'd been knocked out by Mike Tyson. I was trembling inside, my heartbeat raced wildly, like a fox being chased by a thousand bloodhounds. I constantly whispered your name Louise, I felt like a petrified idiot. I wanted to shout your name out loud, but my dry throat had closed up; I was paralysed with fear you see, filled with terror. I thought about jumping in to save you, I stepped close to the edge, but I chickened out when it came to the crunch.

So, I went looking for your folks instead, but I couldn't find them anywhere. I guess they were both at the fish and chip shop, getting ready for a busy days work. I really thought you were on your way to heaven, Louise. Then, something very unexpected happened! A mysterious figure came swishing down on a black aerodynamic flying surfboard, and with no hesitation at all, the figure dived-in and saved you; it was a spectacular rescue, very cool indeed. Now, the unusual thing about this 'spooky-sky-surfer' was their appearance, it wasn't actually a person, just THE SHADOW of a person, crazy hey? A dark shadow and nothing else. I didn't really give this too much thought at the time, cos you were being saved, and that was all that mattered to me, but looking back, I must say, the circumstances were very extraordinary." Richie went on, "This shadow was angry and hostile. It pulled you out of the water and threw you down to the ground like an old rag doll. I still had these huge waves of fear in my tummy, so I decided to run and hide behind some overgrown rose bushes, and keeping very still, I watched the last stage of the rescue unfold. Like a magician, the shadow produced a handful of bright sparkling dust out of nothing, it was all glittery blue, like crushed diamonds... And you were still away with the fairies Louise, sleeping like a baby, completely unconscious, lying back on the hard frosty grass with your face tilted up towards the cold grey sky.

I knew you were still alive, I saw these tiny clouds of mist blowing out from your nostrils, your skin was a stone cold frozen grey-blue mountain-rock face colour, and your lips were dark purple, you looked totally wasted Cuz." Richie took a deep breath. "Holding my breath, I silently watched the shadow grab you, it firmly rubbed the sparkly dust all over your head, and you suddenly woke up with a drunk squiggly smile on your face, your heavy eyelids were all puffed-up, you looked like a dazed circus clown completely drunk on cider. Once all the shampooing was done, the shadow carelessly dropped you like a bad habit, and quickly zoomed back up into the cold gloomy sky. SCHOOOOOOM! And that was it, he was gone. You were coughing and choking big-time now, so I quickly took you back indoors to warm you up, and after ten seconds you threw up, then you rushed upstairs to your bedroom, and puked again, all over your pet hamster Gus, ha-ha." Yep, that's how Richie saw it. I believe this actually happened y'know, that weird magic dust changed me forever! It turned my brown hair blue and made it extra thick. It must've been magic, cos my blue hair now seems to know how to store oxygen inside it, I can breathe underwater for ages now, it's quite weird, but I kind of like it. It's pretty cool I guess, but every time I go for a haircut, it turns out to be a complete nightmare; my thick blue hair destroys the hairdresser's scissors every time. Whoops-a-daisy!

And I tell ya, those fancy hairdressing scissors don't come cheap, they're pretty damn expensive, y'know.
One Italian hairdresser said, "Mamma Mia, it's-a like-a tryin' to cut-a through-de-barbed-wire!" He's got a point, my hair is ridiculously strong these days, kind of like fat heavy acoustic steel guitar strings. That cool Italian dude actually banned me from the hair salon! Can you believe that? These days, whenever I need a trim, I just walk down to the garden shed and dig out the old rusty loppers, using a rubber band I tie my hair back in a ponytail, and chop the big blue waggy tail off, one big snip, and it's all done, no fussin about whatsoever. Sometimes I take the time to trim all the messy bits away, I give it my best shot to create a 'Louise Brooks' Hollywood style bob. I call it the Louise Buttersky blue bob, ha-ha!

So, who was that super-freak on the surfboard?
And why did he, or she, save me?
Will I ever get to meet the weirdo in person, and say thanks for saving my life?
Will I ever get to discover what they're all about?
A big sweeping 'YES' is the answer to all those questions. You see, this bizarre little episode was just the beginning of all my peculiar adventures, more crazy stuff happens to me just a little further down the road, please keep reading my friend, and all shall be revealed.

CHAPTER 2

FLYING HIGH

A few calm years passed without any crazy madness going down, but when I got to the age of eight, something 'Cuckoo' happened to me, it was the middle of summer. I was on a Devon beach with Mum and Dad, when I saw this strange man looking after several massive hot air balloons, they were real big mamas! I could barely see the guy, he was standing way over yonder, down at the far end of the bay. He had a massive sign that said, 'HOT AIR BALLOON RIDES, £20 A POP.' Dad always wanted to go up in a hot air balloon, and this looked like the perfect opportunity to do so, he wanted me to come along for the ride, but I wasn't having any of it. I didn't want to be stuck in the sky, standing inside one of those dodgy old wicker baskets, I guess that kind of thing just ain't my bag. I'm a water baby, a Pisces girl. I'd rather be surfing the waves on my boogie board, secretly breathing underwater with my cool blue hair, I love doing that. So, Mum got dragged into it instead. "We won't be long," said Dad. He wore dark brown shades with red swimming trunks. He would have looked pretty cool, with his handsome face and suave ways, but the big spoiler was his humungous beer belly, it made him look like he was eight and a half months pregnant, sad but true. In *his* mind, Dad thought he was someone cool like James Bond or Indiana Jones, but in reality he looked more like a chubby Elvis from 1977. Dad made me laugh; his ego was way too big. Mum, on the other hand, was a peach. She wore a tiny orange bikini under a white T-shirt, her black trendy retro sunglasses looked dope, she reminded me a little bit of Audrey Hepburn. Mum's always been a head-turner. I kept a casual eye on my folks as they lazily walked off down the beach, holding hands they strolled over to the other side of the bay, I watched Dad pay the old guy, and soon after that, they were up in the sky drifting across the ocean. Well, I immediately knew something was up, I had this dark yukky feeling swirling about inside my solar plexus, it refused to go away, you can probably guess what happened next right? Every time I looked up at my folks I kept having to squint my eyes, so I quickly put my round John-Lennon-style sunglasses on, and that's when I saw them go. It looked as though Mum and Dad were being sucked-up to the very top of the sky, by some dark evil force. "Hey, where are you going?" I shouted and waved. "Come back down!" I pleaded, but they couldn't hear me – they were flying way too high, then they disappeared. Sweet Jesus! What the hell was this!? This truly was a sad-tragic day for me. Remember, I was only eight. The departure of my folks filled my whole body up with deep horrific feelings of abandonment. I felt terrible. I was absolutely heartbroken.

My first reaction was to look over to the strange balloon man and blame him, but he was already gone; the twisted old git magically disappeared into thin air, something sneaky was going on here all right. That was the last time I ever saw my folks, sweet lord, this personal tragedy really messed me up. It felt like my heart got sliced into four pieces, just like a pizza, and two slices got snatched away, right under my nose, and I love pizza. I felt all broken-up inside, emotionally drained, I was absolutely gutted man! I went back home and cried in bed for two whole weeks. I was so upset and lonely. Huge invisible waves of emotional pain took over my whole body, it was such a heavy feeling, and it sucked so bad! I lost all hope, but as the weeks passed, I slowly began to build my strength back up, deep inside I soon found the will to carry on living. The toughest part of all this was having to grow up fast, that was no fun at all, but I had no choice did I? I had to quickly learn how to take care of myself. I still went to school, I did all the ironing, all the shopping, the gardening, all the washing, all the cooking, I fed the rabbits and the goldfish; I even paid the frickin' gas bills. Dad's fish and chip shop closed down; that was a sad day. It was a good thing we still had a pile of cash stored away from the bank job. I kept it hidden under the floorboards in my bedroom, I had twelve shoeboxes full of fifties. At least I wasn't poor, that cheered me up a bit. I can safely say that…the worst part of all this, was the awful feeling of being alone, that gloomy emotion followed me everywhere. I kept in touch with my cousin Richie, on the phone, but that was just once a week. I needed someone to hang out with, someone to play with, someone to come home to, someone to turn to, someone to love me, it was difficult trying to make friends at school, my blue hair seemed to freak the other kids out; I was the weirdo who sat all alone at lunch time. I felt so lost inside. I want to tell you a tiny tale about my folks now, a quickie that'll make you smile, when I was seven and a half, Dad sat me down and told me how much he truly loves Mum, he said that all he wants to do with his life is keep loving me, and Mum. How cool is that? I decided to ask Dad about their wedding, I wanted to know exactly when they got married, and how big a deal it was, I wanted to know if there were lots of people at the reception. Well, the answer I got was completely unexpected, with a reluctant feeling, Dad kind of half-smiled, then he decided to tell me the truth. Taking me back to the VW Beetle-bank-job-day, he gently explained how they both entered the bank as an engaged couple, that's right, at that particular time they weren't even married, but when they held the bank up, there just so happened to be an Irish priest in the queue, I guess he was making a deposit. That's when a crazy idea popped into Dad's waco banana brain. He cracks me up. He told Mum to hold the fort and wait for sixty seconds while he shot across the street to hold up the jewellers, and stealing just one beautiful white-gold diamond ring, he took it straight back to the bank, and while they kept busy filling up their huge bin liners with cash, he got the priest to marry them. They used fake names of course, he told the priest to address them as Bonnie and Clyde, and they got hitched! And that's why they were so crazy-happy when they both jumped back in the car. They were newly-weds who now had tons of cash, ha-ha! Crazy kids! I missed Mum and Dad so much. It was impossible for me to hold my tears back, for months and months, I cried myself to sleep every night. My only comfort was music, every day I played Dad's favourite song on his old cd player, he loved a 1968 hit single called, 'Albatross,' it's an instrumental piece of music recorded by a band called Fleetwood Mac. I played it over and over. It's a soothing tune, it helped calm my nerves. Oh yeh, I almost forgot, there's another track Dad absolutely loves to play, a song called, 'Be My Baby,' by The Ronettes. He loves 'sixties music' so much. Listening to these old tracks gave me a little bit of comfort inside. I needed a great deal of time to recover, my spirit and soul were absolutely crushed, this was a very difficult time for me, real hardship days, but what doesn't kill you makes you stronger right? That old saying turns out to be a 'true-blue-Betty-boo' fact. Ha-ha!

CHAPTER 3

A BLESSING IN DISGUISE

Two difficult years went by, and I was now approaching my tenth birthday, which is on the tenth of March, but on the sixth of March I got caught up in an unexpected domestic pickle. It all happened on a Sunday night, in the kitchen. I was standing by the sink, washing some dishes, when BOOM! The washing machine blew up! It made such a loud bang, it felt like a frickin' bomb had just gone off. I jumped an inch off the ground, while bits of metal flew everywhere. The washing machine door flew over the kitchen table like a wild killer-frisbee. It clipped my ear as it swished and smashed through the big kitchen window, knocking the neighbour's cat off the front garden fence. I never heard Stanley meow like that before. Using a dustpan and brush, I quickly swept up all the broken glass and tossed it in the bin, then I fetched my dad's wheelbarrow from the garage, I put all the broken washing machine parts in it, then I gathered all my half-washed soggy school clothes and dumped them in the big white fireclay sink, they were soaked right through. After mopping-up, I quickly nailed some temporary wood over the smashed window, anyone walking past the cottage now would have probably thought that some kind of crazy old thug was living inside, but it was just little old me. This incident turned out to be a massive inconvenience for me. I needed my uniform washed and ready for school. I had to act fast, so I quickly stuffed my wet heavy school clothes into an old postman's sack, and made a trip into town, I had to find a laundromat fast. Well, there was only one I could think of, the big pink washeteria on the seafront. Our town was a beautiful place in the summer, the beach was always overflowing with families and holidaymakers, lots of people slowly cooking their skin under the sun, just lazing about, soaking up the mellow vibes. Some folks went out canoeing all day, some braved the cold sea for a dip and a paddle, some had their own little beach huts, parking their bums in sun-loungers they'd read books and magazines, lick ice-cream, drink tea, munch on cakes and sandwiches. They seemed to spend the whole summer just chatting away with family, getting toasty brown under the sun. Lots of Daddies in deck chairs scratching their fat hairy sunburnt bellies, with their dogs panting away, sitting in the shade, under the deckchair, lots of fidgety kids with sunblock on their faces, a few tattooed sunbathing daughters, and lots of mellow grandparents, slowly dying in the sun. I remember how everyone loved eating fish and chips, Dad's shop was always busy. Well, that sunny world seemed a million miles away now, outside it was cold, bleak and gloomy, with dark drizzly charcoal skies, typical March weather.

Two minutes after leaving the cottage, I found myself struggling with the heavy postman's sack, so I decided to quickly pop back home and put Dad's wheelbarrow to use. I quickly tipped all the broken washing machine parts out on the back patio, the wheelbarrow was filthy, I hosed it down before chucking my clothes in.

I looked so damn silly walking into town, picture it now, a little girl with blue hair out in the evening rain, pushing a wheelbarrow down the street filled with dirty washing, I looked bonkers, but I didn't care. I quickly got out to the seafront and noticed how dull everything looked, it was like being in a ghost town. Nobody was around, and I mean nobody, I suddenly saw the laundromat 'glowing' over yonder. It was the very last shop on a parade of about twenty shops. I walked past the sweet shop, the toy shop, the beach shop, the toffee shop, the American Diner, the souvenir shop, the tea shop, the bikini shop, the Italian restaurant, the pet shop, the fudge shop, the biscuit shop, the ice cream shop, the fossil shop, the bakery, the Indian restaurant, the English cafe, the candy floss shop, the cake shop, the candle shop, the international coffee shop, the canoe shop, the milkshake shop, and the local dentist, all closed. Only the laundromat was open for business. Oh hang-on, the old pizza and greasy kebab place was lit up too, those guys are always open. I'll never forget my first visit to this 'retro-looking' laundromat, it changed my life forever. Now, as far as laundrettes go, this place was nice. Looking through a tiny clear patch in the steamy window, I could see that it was very well kept, everything looked pristine, shiny and squeaky clean; the whole place was spotless. As I approached the front door, I suddenly noticed a rare and exotic flower sitting on a table, it had a sign beneath it saying: ONE OF A KIND DRAGON-FIRE DAFFODIL FOR SALE. PERFECT FOR HEATING THE HOUSE UP! That sounded a bit 'whip-side-Sally' to me – I guess it was a tropical flower of some kind, it looked like FIRE that wasn't moving. Stepping inside, I immediately felt the heat oozing out from this one-of-a-kind daffodil. It was like walking into the Sahara desert; the place was oven hot. I quickly took my coat off and pushed the heavy glass door right back, making sure it stayed wide open. The cold night air followed me in and helped cool the place down, nobody was around, so I did as I pleased. Leaving Dad's wheelbarrow outside, I speedily stuffed all my clothes into one of the extra large ultra-clean washing machines, I slammed the round door, put some coins and powder in at the top, pushed the 'long-hot-wash' button, stepped back, released a big sigh, and parked my bum on one of the pink plastic chairs. All the other washing machines were empty, I felt like 'Billy-No-Mates' sitting in that lonely laundromat all by myself. I had the Wham-Bam-Yada-Bing-Bang-Blues running through my veins.

Breathing in some fresh sea breeze, I started to relax, I watched my clothes spin around and around. I still felt terribly sad about my absent folks, I just felt so heavy inside, like my heart was wrapped in chains. I ended up singing the blues. Billy-No-Mates? I felt more like Billie Holiday. A big gust of wind suddenly blew into the shop, and it almost knocked me off my seat. It must have been travelling over the ocean at two hundred miles an hour. This bold 'Windrush' filled my lungs; it was beautiful. After closing my eyes and taking a few deep breaths, I had a strange feeling come over me, like something mischievous was lurking in the air. It was the kind of wobbly sensation one feels just before an electric thunderstorm kicks off, silent invisible electric menacing vibrations slowly growing in the atmosphere. Then I got distracted, all my attention suddenly got drawn to the sound of a delightful singing voice, it came from just outside the shop. It's volume grew louder and bolder, and that's when I saw her - this beautiful woman confidently walked into the laundromat like she was walking out onto a stage in Las Vegas, she looked like a cosmic pop star. She was stunningly beautiful, 'She must be the boss,' I whispered to myself, an eccentric animated lady, bright and bubbly all over, anyone could tell she was a positive soul. This radiant babe seemed to have big happy feelings bursting out from her heart, spilling in all directions. Her presence seemed to glow with sweet satori bliss, her vibe was fresh and fizzy, like pink frothy lemonade. Maybe she was a Sagittarius, or perhaps a Pisces-girl like me. She was holding a brand new mop in her hand, but to her, it was a 'pretend' microphone. In her imagination she was performing a huge power ballad at the Hollywood Bowl. She sung a song called, 'Hit Me With Your Best Shot.' A great track by Pat Benatar. Her unique voice gave me goosebumps all over; she was super talented, she blasted all her emotions right out from the pit of her tummy. I was completely affected by her big spirit, the coolest thing about this woman was the way she seemed to be totally relaxed about everything, nothing rattled her cage, she just flowed along slow and cool like a mellow river, all her actions were effortless. The first thing that caught my eye was her big pink fuzzy hairdo, she had it all fluffed-up like candy floss, it looked quite funny. Her sparkling emerald eyes danced wildly behind a large pair of purple framed glasses, they shined a bright blaze, like big green traffic lights saying… 'Go-Go-Go!' Her skin looked so divine, she had hundreds of rusty-looking freckles sprinkled down her slender arms, they looked like tiny tattoos of autumn leaves, the larger freckles looked like cornflakes dipped in honey, she had perfectly painted lilac fingernails, and her sassy smile seemed to wash ALL BAD THINGS AWAY, My O My, this girl was stunning!

She looked pretty damn fantastic in her blue jeans and white T-shirt, on top of that she wore a big black and yellow stripy apron, she was the prettiest Queen Bee I ever saw. Ha! She had cool sneakers too; white slip-ons with giant plastic sunflowers over the toes, and she stunk of yummy coconut oil, it was a gorgeous subtle fragrance. She caught my presence in the corner of her eye, gave me a quick smile, and suddenly popped back outside to do a spot of singing and dancing in the rain. I found that to be a bold flamboyant move. She was so care-free and happy, she oozed out a natural American 'Tina-Turner-Beyonce-style' stage-confidence, this bella bambina was a pure-solid-back-bone-beauty. A happy-go-lucky-heart-breaker.

If I was singing big, giving it my all, and in a flash, I suddenly realised that I wasn't alone, well, I would have probably stopped in my tracks and curled up like a shy little hedgehog, but not this vivid girl, she was a song blaster. This Laundromat Lady filled me up with curiosity and intrigue. Who was this wacky woman? And why is she so damn happy and enthusiastic about everything? I'd like to have some of that energy in my body, it was magnetic, infectious, impossible to ignore. It was like she had pure sunlight trapped in her heart, and the only way to release it was to sing out loud. Like a wary little tom-cat, I continued watching her every move, she moonwalked to a back room and soon returned with two big baskets full of dirty washing, into the small machines they went, for an express wash, and straight into the big yellow tumble dryers after, she speedily folded all the dry clothes into nice neat piles, she looked like she could have done this with her eyes closed. She was entertaining to watch, she blabbered away constantly, every single thought that passed through her mind automatically popped out of her mouth, she babbled-on and sniggered away about who knows what, then there was silence, before a big belly laugh came out; she was nuts! Her zany nature cheered me up in three seconds, then, without any warning, she spontaneously threw a clean pair of football socks at me, they hit my chest and landed on my lap, she giggled a bit.

"Hey gorgeous, fancy joining me for a nice hot cuppa tea, served with a cheeky slice of lemon sponge cake on the side?" Well, how could I refuse such a sweet kind offer? "Oh yes please, I'd be delighted." Said I. "Yippee! Tea-time with a stranger!" She smiled brightly while skipping and dancing towards the little hatch by the old back room, she reached-in to switch an old metal kettle on, then she slid across the floor, skidding like a zany six year-old she bumped into me and gently shook my hand. "Hi love, my name's Betty." Her hands were ever so soft. "Hi Betty, very nice to meet you, I'm Louise." Lovely bubbly Betty, that's what I whispered to myself. Two minutes later I was attending an old fashioned indoor picnic, Betty used a yellow china tea pot with matching tea cups. We sipped tea, rambled away, and slowly scoffed on our sponge cake slices, the sugary icing gave me a nice little energy boost. We spoke about tropical flowers, washing machine motors and pop stars. Betty said her favourite singers are Cyndi Lauper, Bjork, Kate Bush, Cher and Aretha Franklin. My favourite singers are Tina Turner, Norah Jones and Linda Ronstadt. I turned to look outside, and suddenly noticed how the weather had changed for the worse, the soft drizzly showers had slyly turned into a wild rainy thunderstorm; it was practically on top of us, the wind blew ferociously with no mercy. I saw a fat old lady, holding a pizza box, walk by the shop window, she was singing the national anthem, when her wig suddenly blew off! Ha! A hard rain fell into the shop now, Betty rushed over to close the big front glass door, the shop went all quiet, oh look at that, my long hot wash finally finished, I took my clothes out and threw them into one of the big dryers, this was the moment I suddenly became all sad again. I didn't want to go back to the cottage, it was empty and lonely, nobody was waiting for my return. That place didn't feel like home anymore; it felt more like a flippin' prison. "What's the matter, sweetheart?" Asked Betty. "Why the sad face?" I told her all about the strange way my folks had disappeared at the beach, nearly two years prior, and boldly expressed how lonely I felt. I was trying so hard to be brave and strong, but I just couldn't hold my tears back. I felt like a dopey idiot crying to a beautiful stranger, my intuition told me to be brave and open up to Betty. I knew she had a compassionate spirit, she opened her arms and gave me a tender little squeeze. "Oh dear, it sounds like you've had a pretty rough ride." Locking her arms around me, Betty proceeded to give me the biggest boldest bear hug ever! I almost lost my breath. When she finally backed-up, she closed her eyes tight and sneezed all over my face, then she laughed out loud before making a small announcement. This eccentric vixen was completely unafraid of eye contact, she looked straight into my soul for what seemed like an eternity; those big green beauties hypnotised me, Betty spoke with hearty clarity.

"Ok, listen up, my wounded little lamb, this will probably come-off sounding a bit batty, but I'd like to invite you to stay over for the night. A sleepover y'know."

Betty smiled like Julia Roberts, I felt real love in her voice.

"I adore this beautiful wild storm above us, what with all its glorious thunder and rain and electricity, but I really don't want to be sending you home in it, you'll get soaked right down to your bones, and you'll probably end up catching a cold. So please stay here with me tonight, in my cosy apartment upstairs, you can crash in the spare room and sleep with the angels. Y'know, everything feels better after a good night's sleep, that's a fact of life my dear. I'll wake you up at six, cook you breakfast and send you on your merry way." Betty truly was a sweet, kind, dotty soul. I gazed outside and tried to make my mind up, I guess I was reflecting, the dark heavy mood of the bold storm looming over us felt so intrusive, it sent a quivering 'slow-motion' shiver down my spine. The thunder and lightning sounded like they were fighting over a beautiful woman, and the merciless rain came down like it was it's last performance ever. I slowly sighed, then I said something to myself in the privacy of my own thoughts, "Well Hot Digity Dog, I'm gonna go for it!" That was the moment I turned to Betty and said, "Oh yes please. I'd love to stay over, if that's all right with you?" I felt like I was being too polite now, it's not easy being English y'know, we get self conscious and apologetic over nothing, we can be far too polite and over-courteous without even thinking about it, so many of us say sorry for absolutely no reason at all... Sorry about that, ha-ha. And sometimes, we're far too nice to the most awful people. What's that all about? I guess it's just the way we've been programmed. It's a strange old world, I would improve my programming at the drop of a hat, if I knew how. Betty took a deep breath, she smiled like a happy daffodil in the sun, glowing with amber joy,

"Hip-hip hooray, you've made an excellent choice my love. I'll go make your bed. And of course it's all right with me, I want you to stay over, you silly little rabbit."

And so it happened...We closed the shop up together, switched all the lights off, and moseyed on upstairs to Betty's private pad. This peculiar laundromat lady was quickly growing on me, getting right under my skin she was, in a good way of course. I really liked her a lot. She was a true-blue sweetheart, full of love and vigour. A colourful angel sent to me from the stars above, maybe from the Greek Gods? Who knows? She had a wonderful child-like innocence about her, she was just like 'Clarence' the second class angel, only sharper, do you know that guy? He's the one who saves George Bailey, in that old classic film... 'IT'S A WONDERFUL LIFE!'

That's a great movie! Make sure you check it out.

CHAPTER 4

AN UNEXPECTED WAKE UP CALL

Betty's pad upstairs was lush, a first-class cosy crib. Now, the main thing that caught my eye in her spare room was the huge solid oak bunk bed; it looked so inviting. I quickly climbed-up to the top bunk and got ready for bed. The mattress was super soft, and the brilliant white cotton bedsheets and pillows felt like heaven. The wild storm outside was in full swing now; lots of crazy 'Ocean-Swish' kept bashing itself against the window, I kind of liked it – it made the whole room feel like a safe cocoon. I had a good long look around before switching the big light off. It was impossible to ignore Betty's huge hanging pictures. One was a picture of Niagara Falls, another was a picture of the Grand Canyon, and the one by the big front window was a cool blown up photo of a Californian Redwood tree, with a car driving through it, some of those trees can grow to over a hundred meters tall y'know. That's awesome! As I examined these big glossy pics, I noticed that Betty was in every shot, smiling in the corner of the frame, with a fancy looking ironing board tucked under her arm, she looked like a cosmic surfer-girl. I guess some people go on vacation with travel irons, but when it comes to a star like Betty, she evidently insists on taking her travel-ironing-board along with her too, oh dear, it takes all kinds I guess. She was born to shine. I found all these huge photos to be pretty odd, but I guess Betty is quite an odd and eccentric sort of lady, I decided not to give it too much thought. I felt safe in her presence and that was all that mattered to me, intuition never lies, make sure you remember this. It suddenly dawned on me that I was very tired, so, I hit the lights, said a little prayer, and after ten seconds, I was gone, sound asleep, snoozing away like a relaxed happy bear-cub slipping into hibernation. I fell into a deep transcending slumber, I dreamt I was enjoying a delicious Sunday roast dinner with my folks, but all that quickly changed when I got rudely awakened at two in the morning, by a horribly loud aggressive whacking noise. It sounded like race cars were smashing into each other just outside my window; this awful disturbance bugged the hell out of me, the bedroom walls shook like jelly. One might say it was almost traumatising. Bam! Another huge cracking bazooka blast! I jumped down from the top-bunk and quickly crept into the bed below; all the blankets were stiff and cold. Boom! Another earth-shaking-zippa-whip-blast! I jumped up again and quickly slid and hid under the mattress. I was petrified now! Holy-Sha-Moan! What a horrible way to be woken up. This was far too 'Crazy-Bananas' for me. The bedroom door suddenly burst open, and Betty came rushing-in, she looked like a flustered super-hero who was late for a therapy session, she had this stern serious look on her face, "Get dressed, Louise!

Nice and quickly now – we need to get out of here on the double! She's only gone and found us. I don't know how, but that's definitely her outside." Betty was more serious than happy go lucky.

"Who's found us? What the hell are you talking about? What's going on, Betty?" I asked with genuine passionate shaky concern, cosmic Betty looked right into my eyes.

"Ok, listen up kid. I'll give you the short version now and the long version later. There's a crazy witch outside, and she's here for you. She wants to get a hold of you – big time! There's something you've got, and she wants it!" Betty's voice was deadpan. I knew she was talking straight because I felt these icy shivers run right down my spine; I kind of liked it. I was scared, but at the same time, I felt so alive, shameless fear stirred about inside my little tummy. I was wide awake now.

"A crazy witch? Do what now? This is a joke, right?"

"No, it's not a joke, this is real, but I can tell you a joke if you like. What did Luke Skywalker get for Christmas? Have you felt his presents?" Betty giggled a little bit.

"Why is she after me? I mean, what have I done wrong?" Betty took a deep breath. "Louise, it's hard to explain in a heartbeat ok, I'll give you all the details later, I promise, you have my word, but right now we need to get our cute little cupcakes out of here, I'm talking lightning-speed." Betty pulled her pink ski goggles down over her eyes, and handed a white pair to me.

"Here, put these on," she said. I did what I was told, then I quickly threw my jeans back on. "Oh, lovely," she said.
"The white goggles really compliment your sky-blue hair." My goodness, Betty was too much. We had a psychopathic-waco-witch on our doorstep trying to blow us up, and all she could think about was 'fashion' - crazy lady. While putting my socks and trainers on, I watched Betty get all worked up with some funny dance moves. She took short breaths followed by long deep breaths, then she jumped up and down on the spot, behaving like a hyperactive cheerleader, she performed some tip-top star-jumps, then she started giving herself a pep talk…"Come on baby, come on baby, who's number one? Betty, that's who." She continued jumping about, banging her head on the ceiling a few times. "Take me home, Daddio. Take me back to the Bing-Bang-Boo! Take me back to Scooby-Doo in Timbuktu! Let me be fire, let me be true, I am a samurai sword born to slash right through! Yes Sir!" What the hell was she going on about? Was I dreaming all this or what? Betty was now shaking her hips, and waving her bum around in a slow, groovy 'Rub-A-Dub' style. Sweet Delilah, what have I gotten myself into? I slapped my face a few times, while Betty slipped into a bright red puffy ski jacket, she had a big pink one set aside for me.

"Here Louise, put this puffer jacket on. It's cold outside."

I threw it over my arms and quickly zipped it up, my young-blooded curiosity suddenly dared me to take a quick sneaky peek out the window. HOLY MAMA! There she was, a wild witch loitering about outside. She laughed and coughed with an evil rasp of wickedness in her throat, this crazy old spirit kept perfect balance on a black flying surfboard, it hovered just a few inches above the ground, she had a black velvet bag full of exploding conker bombs. Bam! She threw another one into the shop, these malicious banger-bombs made huge cracks in the walls. This was the most insane morning ever! This witchy weirdo was a twisted sicko, she had these big red eyeballs that sizzled like hot lumps of coal. Pulling me away from the window, Betty took me downstairs, and rushing past all the washing machines we headed straight for the small back-room. Betty karate-kicked the 'staff-only' door down, she dragged me into what looked like a dusty old boiler room, it was filled with junk, there was a tiny old rickety wooden kitchen table, a black kettle, a red wooden stool, a huge 'Jailhouse Rock' Elvis poster on the wall, over thirty rusty old broken down ironing boards scattered everywhere, an old TV, an old VHS video cassette player, and two Walmart shopping trollies filled with spare oily washing machine parts. Betty quickly ripped the carpet up and got busy unlocking a secret trap door, it had four chunky padlocks. Betty used her unique key-shape earrings to unlock them. I thought this was our escape route, but how wrong I was. Betty opened the trap door and quickly pulled out a massive supersonic ironing board, it was completely futuristic, a high cut above all the surrounding tatty boards, it was the same fancy one in all the photos, it had a huge twin-pack-rocket-engine attached to its underbelly. Betty started it up like a lawnmower, she threw it down to the ground where it hummed and hovered quietly, it kept still, behaving like a well-trained dog waiting to be told what to do. "This is my jet-powered rocket ironing board, Louise. It's our safe ticket out of here." Keeping perfect balance, Betty hopped-up onto the board like a confident sassy pussy cat. "It's time for you and I to hit the skies my love, we need to see what this wild-little-speed-racer can do, are you in?"

"You bet your sweet cheeks I'm in." I said.

"Oh, jolly good show. Jump up here and wrap your arms around my waist, I'm gonna take you for a ride that's gonna blow your brain into another dimension. Just make sure you hold on tight, ok honey." Betty suddenly pulled a whistle out of her pocket, and with all her passion she blew on it as hard as she could. "All aboard!" She giggled. I quickly hopped up and threw both my arms around her darling figure. "Tickets, please," she giggled even louder now. "Oh stop being silly will ya, come on, let's go. Let's get out of here!" I was beginning to freak out a little bit.

"Sure thing little lady, HOLD ON TO YOUR KNICKERS!"

The rocket board suddenly made a huge majestic rumbling sound, it roared and revved-up like a wild angry dragster car, getting ready to blast off into outer space.

"Here we go, baby!" Betty was so happy about all this, she was like a stunt woman, eager to get flirting with some serious danger. SCHOOOOOOOOOOOOOOOM!!!

Like a bullet from a gun, we zoomed past all the washing machines and smashed right through the laundromats big glass door. In passing, Betty gave the horrible witch a good firm slap on the face, this truly got her riled up; boy-o-boy, she was proper-loco-livid now. Pure volcanic witch anger! "Chase me, you old slag-bag!" Shouted Betty.

We raced up into the night-time sky like a blazing hot firework, before I could blink we were already flying out over the Atlantic Ocean. My goodness, that rocket ironing board was shifty. It had a whole lotta horse-power. This was the moment I realised that Betty was a true-blue-wild-hearted-danger-loving-dare-devil-kamikaze-waco-whizz-kid! She was probably born year of the Tiger, or Dragon.

"Never grow up, Louise! Never let yourself become old and boring. There's just too much fun to be had. Ha-Ha!"

The old girl's right you know. Betty was bold, brave and fearless. A fierce, feisty fire-angel, full of substance, a true adrenaline junkie, a wild gipsy spirit hooked on danger, she was ready to rumble, and I was coming along for the ride, with no safety-belt, just my firm faithful grip. Yikes! I quickly looked over my shoulder, to see how far ahead we were. Now, the only thing I saw behind us were two red dots in our slipstream, they looked like a lorry hitting the brakes down a dark country lane, but they soon got bigger. That batty old witch was gaining on us fast, her big bulging eyes glowed like two red-hot tennis balls made from volcano lava. The determination of this evil spirit was very intimidating, her aggressive morbid energy had a magnetic pull to it, it was like a vacuum cleaner trying to suck me in, and she was still throwing those lethal conker bombs; sweet lord, she had such a nerve. Both Betty and the witch kept amazing balance as they surfed through the night-time sky. I was absolutely blown away by all this night-time madness, I had so much strange energy racing through me, all the adrenaline zapping through my little body felt fantastic. I wee'd in my knickers, just a tiny bit. We suddenly flew past some Canadian geese, Betty turned to me and said, "Hey Louise, welcome to your first wild goose chase, ha-ha!" She laughed out loud like she didn't have a care in the world, she was crackers! Y'know, sometimes, I used to daydream and wonder about how it might feel to fly alongside Superman. Well, now I know exactly how it feels. It's totally exhilarating! An awesome tip-top rush! Ha-ha. Thanks Betty. This intense sky-ride made American-rollercoaster-big-dipper-rides feel like a Sunday picnic in the park, sincerely. The chase was on!

CHAPTER 5

THE CRAZY CHASE

This crazy chase really was a fat chunky slice of intense madness. The obsessed witch followed us like a possessed Terminator, maybe she was the Terminator's Grandmother? I tried to take my mind off the current situation by checking out all the beautiful night-time scenery above, over a million bright stars silently watched over us, they glimmered in the reflection of the ocean too, shining magnificently like sacred angels. I guess the heavy thunderstorm from the night before had rolled-on down to Spain, or Africa maybe. It was nice surfing through the night-time sky, but it would have been nicer if we had more time on our hands. Sky-surfing at top speed, on a rocket ironing board is an extremely nerve-racking and dangerous sport, I was trying my best not to throw up, the stargazing helped. We flew at ridiculous speeds, slashing through the skies like a couple of bazooka rockets. I held on to Betty's waist with all the strength I could muster. Oh no! We suddenly flew straight into the heart of a scoopy air pocket. Hooooo-wee! We got pushed and bullied about by some tricky hardcore turbulence, then a wild jagged jolt of G-force wind suddenly threw us back, and I accidentally puked-up some lemon sponge cake mixed with cold tea, whoops a daisy, please don't tell anyone about this. I hope it landed on that witches face, ha-ha! The crazy old hag!

I was feeling pretty dizzy now, all out of sync, the ironing board flipped and danced all over the place, it moved like it had the hiccups, the next surprise was my legs getting swooped out from underneath me, they flapped and kicked away like crazy ribbon-tassels tied to a kid's bike. I had an obscene amount of adrenaline dancing in my heart now. Holy Macaroni! My hands were so damn sweaty, I'm not sure how I did it, but I somehow managed to improve my grip around Betty's waist, I locked both my hands together, interlacing my fingers - making one big fist, this was crazy. I tried to sort my legs out next. Betty suddenly performed a quick manoeuvre that helped, she flew up to a higher altitude, this quick slick trick helped me get my feet back on the board. After that close shave, I knelt down and squeezed the board with all my strength, it felt much safer crouching low under Betty's legs. I'm sure I heard her singing to herself, the loud volume of the constant howling wind made it difficult for me to recognise the song she was shouting. I think it was AC-DC, 'Shook Me All Night Long.' The higher we flew, the colder it got, thank God for those big ski-jackets, the goggles were pretty awesome too. Thanks to the full moon above, I saw everything below us with a clear view, the moon provided a nice icy blue light, there wasn't much to see, just our shadows dashing along the big bold glittery ocean surface. Check out this shot of me and Betty, it was taken by a Russian satellite. Cheese!

Looking just in front of me, I saw that the ironing board had a mini sat-nav system built into its digital speedometer. Holy smoke, we were travelling at 1750 mph! Is that possible? This was completely nuts! But it sure was a lot of fun. The power of our speed pulled all the skin on my face right back, this would have been a great ride for old people looking for a face-lift. The sound of the thunderous wind blew ferociously in my ears; it felt like a frick'in hurricane was trying to break into my mind. Imagine sticking your head out the window of a super sonic race car, while killing it along the Utah Bonneville Salt Flats. Youser! I turned my head to have another quick look behind us, and there she was, still on our tail, those crazy crimson eyes glowed with rage. This witch meant business; she was no slouch, she was so determined to catch us, and get us. Betty was right about the ride, it was, without a doubt, blowing my brain into another dimension. I suddenly heard Betty's voice in my head, just as we approached America.

"Next stop, New York City." Betty had this unique ability to communicate with me through her thoughts; it was a strange talent, but a pretty neat trick. I looked out in front and saw all the buildings of New York City lined up ahead, then I saw the Statue of Liberty beneath us, we dashed past her torch in half a second. Betty proceeded to fly straight into the heart of downtown Manhattan, cutting and weaving through all the high-rise buildings. The red-eyed psycho witch followed close behind, I suddenly noticed a big green button on the ironing board's control pad. It had two big words printed on it: 'LONDON FOG.' Betty quickly communicated a direct 'thought-order' to me. "Hit the green button, Louise!" That was all I heard. So I quickly reached over and pushed the big button down as fast as I could, then I went back to bear-hugging the ironing board, I didn't fancy falling down into the streets below, no way.

Now, what happened next was, by a long shot, one of the

coolest things I have ever seen. The jet-powered rocket board's ironing exhaust pipe spat out huge amounts of thick mist, it was pure London fog, and after maybe forty seconds, the whole of Manhattan was completely covered by a huge blob of smoky London smog. It was the biggest cloud ever, and it made the perfect hiding place. We slipped into the fog-blob and gently hovered around inside. Everything suddenly became super silent, I heard the crazy witch follow us in. I tell ya man, this fog was so thick, I couldn't even see my hand when I held it up in front of me. I suddenly heard a low-pitched gutsy snorting kind of sound, it was the heavy breathing of the psycho-fudge-brain-waco-witch. Sweet Jaffa Cakes, she was right beside us, oh my days! I kept completely still.

"Don't breathe," said Betty, in her thought mode.

This thought communication technique turned out to be pretty useful, especially for a sticky jam like this one, it only works when the person is right beside you, well, that's what Betty said, anyway. I felt the witch's bad vibrations lurk all around us, dark sinister feelings, I heard her busy nose sniffing about. Her putrid breath was disgusting; it smelt like fox poo mixed with sour milk, I was trying so hard not to heave, to escape the foul stench, I quickly tucked my face deep into my jacket, this awful witchy woman had the nature of a grumpy old goblin ghoul, she was rotten right down to the core. She took short breaths and belched constantly, she sounded like a pug-dog having an asthma attack, and she coughed like a cigar munching pig. I picked up a new scent now, it was the stench of her foul body odour, oh my lord, she stunk like a poor old tramp sleeping out on the streets of London, a pissy jeans kind of smell. She badly needed a hot bleach bath. Sorry for swearing. This felt like a very intense game of hide and seek, we kept so still, pausing like two shrewd foxes hiding in the woods, just waiting for the right moment to make our move. Betty slipped her arm around my waist and gently whispered six 'thought-words' to me: "Hold tight, honey. Here we go." The jet-powered rocket ironing board suddenly revved-up like a wild chainsaw, we blasted away from that foggy cloud like a bat out of hell, and headed straight back to old England, this time the ironing board picked-up even more speed. Seconds after swishing past the Empire State building, Betty telepathically communicated a thought idea to me. "Lie down flat on the board, Louise. We'll get back to England much faster this way." So I did just that, and Betty laid on top of me; this made us more aerodynamic, we moved so fast, like a human bullet. I was lying down flat, with the digital speedo screen right in my face, I hugged that board like a stunned Koala bear. Heading back home, we reached a top speed of 2555 miles per hour, yeah baby, this was totally awesome! Speed is my new best friend. Ha-ha. I wasn't all that keen on getting left behind, so I squeezed that board with ALL my strength, but my grip just wasn't strong enough, the fierce G-force was too powerful, I ended-up getting sucked out from under Betty's body. I got swooped away by the lethal fire force around us, I was left far behind now, free-falling in the middle of the sky, floating aimlessly above the Atlantic Ocean, falling fast towards the freezing cold sea below. I saw my whole life flash before me, the years swooped by in three seconds. I was just two inches away from hitting the cold ocean surface when… SCHWIIIIIING! Betty came back just in the nick of time, she made an ultra-fast supersonic U-turn, and snatched me right out of the sky, one of my trainers actually dipped into the ocean. Holy guacamole! That was spicy. I thought Betty was gonna slow down after that close shave, but NO! She didn't hold back at all. She got back up to crazy speeds in a flash, but this time she zipped me up inside her jacket, that was a cool move. We overtook five aeroplanes after that; I heard their engines screaming wildly as we swished on by. This whole experience felt like a crazy dream, we were probably travelling close to the speed of light, maybe, I don't know. Our trip back to Devon gave me an abundance of endorphins. It made me forget all about my troubles back home, I wasn't feeling sad, blue or lonely, hell no, far from it. I actually felt great inside. I was 'living-large' baby. No extra baggage on my back-burner. We got back to Devon super quick, and the crazy old witch was nowhere to be seen, my god I was so pleased about that. Betty had tears in her eyes when she saw the state of her pink seafront laundromat; the crazy witch smashed it up real good. It looked like a bomb site, this was a heartbreaking sight to see. It used to be such a beautiful washeteria, Betty seemed to shrug it all off and move on pretty fast, there was no time to be grieving over material things. "We need to get over to the tumble dryers," she whispered. "Why? Have you got some washing you need to finish?" I asked.

"No, silly," she giggled. "I have an escape plan."

"Ah, ok, sounds good." I looked down and suddenly saw the beautiful dragon-fire daffodil, lying 'pot-less' on the floor. I quickly picked it up and handed it to Betty, it wasn't even warm now. I guess it only turns hot when it's in soil.

Looking around, I saw that all the washing machines and all the big yellow tumble dryers were totally smashed up. Those destructive conker-bombs were like hand grenades, the witch probably threw a bunch of them into the shop just after we left, oh dear. I suddenly heard some low heavy creaking sounds, it felt like the whole building was going to collapse any second. Hopping back on the rocket board, we quickly flew over to the last tumble dryer, the one that sat all by itself, at the back, by the kitchen hatch door, it had sticker tape all over it that said,

'OUT OF ORDER.' Betty quickly ripped the tape off, opened the big round door, and gently flew the both of us in. "Hey, what's this all about?" I asked.

"You'll see in a moment," to avoid banging her pink head, Betty crouched over me, softly ploughing her chin into my thick blue hair she said, "Not everything is as it seems, my love." "You're telling me," I said. Betty's lively voice was a little more relaxed now, her soothing calming energy rubbed off on me, and I must say, I was very pleased to receive it. It was a great feeling, knowing that there was no immediate danger around us. This big old tumble dryer looked like a normal machine from the outside, but once inside, a little light flicked on, and a kind of submarine porthole door opened at the back, well hoochie mama what have we got here? The open door led us into a secret tunnel, it was an extremely long tunnel that led all the way back to Betty's other laundrette, up in West London. "We're not safe here in Devon anymore, Louise. We need to stay one step ahead of… you know who, so I'm gonna take you to my West London laundromat cave; it's a good place to hide out." I picked up the raw urgent love in Betty's voice. "Ok, let's do it!" I was enjoying this adventure, and I didn't want to hit the brakes, bring on the next challenge I say, it felt safer and wiser to keep moving. I didn't want to be a sitting rubber ducky for that psycho witch to prey on, no way Jose. The more distance we had between us and that red-eyed-psycho-rat-face-freak, the better. She seemed to have pure evil energy in her blood, she was a rancid disgusting old cow. Betty started to explain a few things, as we slowly cruised along the narrow tunnel, "My secret hide-out cave sits directly under my West London laundromat, about fifty meters below ground level. We'll be safe down there. For a while anyway." "Sounds good to me Betty-Boo. Let's keep rolling." So off we went to London. After fifteen minutes of tunnel travel, Betty patted me on the back and said, "Hey Louise, check this out." She pushed a little red button on her Casio calculator watch that quickly detonated a huge 'Self-destruct-bomb,' hidden inside the basement, back at the old Devon laundromat. We heard and felt the huge explosion echo right behind us, it ricocheted down the tunnel, the severe vibrations felt like a mini earthquake. Betty's seaside laundromat was history now, all that was left was a huge pile of rubble and junk.

"If you're going to do a job, do it properly," Betty snapped her fingers and laughed out loud. "Oh well, it was a lovely laundrette, never mind, onwards and upwards, mustn't dwell on the past." Betty's sadness for the loss of her laundromat was very fleeting, I was quite impressed with the way she seemed willing to just shrug it off, all in the space of about ten seconds, just a splash of water off a duck's back, not too shabby at all, nice one Betty. She's got to be a Sagittarius, her heart was full of fire, and she obviously loves to travel, pretty damn fast I might add. The good news was this: we had successfully covered our tracks, the entrance to the secret tunnel was now buried under a huge pile of steel beams, roof tiles, old bricks, and smashed up washing machines. Betty suddenly coughed as she readied herself to talk some more,

"Hey Louise, I can safely say that we won't be coming back tomorrow to collect your school clothes. Ha ha!"

Betty had a very mischievous laugh, it echoed right down the tunnel, and after ten minutes, the echo boomeranged its way back up towards us, and we laughed some more.

It took longer than I thought to get to London, about two and a half hours. Betty flew with great skill and dexterity, she carefully manoeuvred the jet-powered rocket ironing board through all the narrow 'breathe-in-tight' bottleneck bits, we were ducking and diving the morning away. She was only doing about a hundred miles an hour, many times she ducked my head down for me. We finally arrived. Yes! Sitting on that jet board for two and a half hours wasn't exactly travelling business class. I was hunched and crouched over like an old granny, knitting a scarf. I felt stiff all over, like a scarecrow. It felt great to finally stand up straight and shake my legs about, I had a good long stretch, and so did Betty. She kicked her shoes off, brushed her teeth, and flicked her purple kettle on. I was intrigued by the mighty strange collection of weird stuff she'd accumulated down in her hideout cave – I will get to all that in a minute. Still holding her toothbrush in her mouth, Betty kept busy sorting out her dragon-fire daffodil. Pinching some soil from her unique bonsai tree collection, she replanted the daff in a huge coffee mug, adding just a humble measure of tap water. "I'll take this lovely flower up to my London laundrette tomorrow; it needs sunlight." Betty looked like she'd just gotten out of bed, her pink punky hair was more fluffed-up than usual, pure-fuzz-mania, this made me smile; she looked like a 70's glam-rock David Bowie fan. When the kettle boiled, Betty slowly poured herself a nice hot cup of green tea, I got a cold glass of fresh pineapple juice, it was lovely. We plonked ourselves down in the two brown armchairs that sat in the middle of the cave. At last, we had some free time to soak up some peace and quiet.

"You can go back to bed now, if you like," The life-energy in Betty's bright green eyes quickly revealed the unbreakable spirit in her heart, she suddenly laughed out loud, like a rich happy queen. Laughter was by far the best medicine for us to fill our bodies with, it helped us dissolve all the stress we'd absorbed back in New York.

"The key to successful living is to be like Keith Richards, laugh every day, and stay relaxed." That's what Betty kept saying, before singing another song, down in the tunnel. She lived like anadolescent gipsy Jedi-warrior, one who liked to stay up late. Our spirits chilled as we slowly unwound, and after maybe seven or eight minutes Betty stood up straight and said,

"Louise, I fancy a quick shower; I feel stinky all over. I need to freshen up."

"Sure thing," I said.

Humming a happy little tune, Betty walked into her tiny en-suite-shower-cave and quickly stripped off. I remained seated in the comfy old brown leather armchair, I gave it my best shot to have a go at meditating for ten minutes, but my wild speeding heartbeat left me feeling quite restless and fidgety, it ticked away like crazy techno music, much faster than its usual rhythm.

Anyway, I couldn't keep my eyes closed to save my life, there was too much good stuff to look out in Betty's hideout cave, it was jam-packed full of gems and gadgets and goodies. I'll give you a run-down on all that in a minute.

This hideout cave was really cool, it was the kind of place Batman would take Cat-woman for coffee and kisses, after seeing the latest Spiderman movie down at the local cinema, a nice secret place to 'make-out' and have a good smooch.

CHAPTER 6

THE TRUTH WILL SET YOU FREE

It was the perfect time for me to get extra nosey down in Betty's extraordinary cave, the whole place was rammed to the rim, filled with interesting gear, I'm guessing the beautiful pink-headed tomboy was a secret hoarder, my eyes wandered all over, it was like being inside a secret underground emporium, filled with tip-top freaky junk. I decided to have a good snoopy-snoop, while the freckly candy-floss-head sang in the shower. Here's a list of what I saw in the cave: Seventeen old witches' broomsticks, an old white skateboard carved out from a T-Rex dinosaur fang, a pair of turbo-powered roller skates (fully equipped with mini nitro-rockets), an automatic robotic metal detector, with flippers and fins (you can drop it in the ocean and it will return with gold pieces), there were two pink wetsuits complete with all the best scuba diving gear, an old record player, ten flying ironing boards all with twin rocket-packs. I enjoyed looking at the huge bookshelf made from dinosaur bones, and looking closer, I saw a bowl of rainbow marbles sitting on a pile of dusty old books, next to the bowl was a yellow 'post-it-slip' with a scribbly message that said..."Keep sharp Betty, Live Large, Be Bold, Surf only the brave-waves of life, and make sure you never lose your Bing-Bang-Boo-Marbles! Love from Betty." Holy mackerel, Betty was a nuts! She was a one of a kind, sky-surfing-cosmic-wild-child. A daring, dashing, ding-dong-fire-angel, a very rare breed indeed. Next I saw lots of little wooden shelves fixed up high around the cave, they were filled with old broken rocket engine pistons, and different motor parts. Sitting close to an old washing machine I saw a bashed-up chrome fridge and a shiny jaded vintage cooker, they looked like they'd been dropped out of a twenty storey building, dents and bruises all over, they certainly had a lot of character. After her shower, the green-eyed goddess came out wearing a black and white stripy dressing gown. Her hair looked totally puffed and power-zapped. She looked like a cosmic halloween Beetlejuice bride. Walking over to a blue cupboard, Betty opened the door, grabbed a petrol-powered garden blower and got busy drying and styling her wacky fluffed-up hairdo. "Give us a hand, please love." I was happy to help, spending time with Betty was a unique experience. I pointed the blower right into her boat race, I smiled away as I watched the powerful rushing airstreams wobble her cheeks about, she made all sorts of funny facial expressions. She was like a perfect eccentric auntie, cursed with a spicy appetite for big bad danger. Once her hair was dried, waxed and styled, she slipped into her jeans, threw a clean T-shirt on and sat back down in the old squeaky brown leather armchair, I decided to park my bum back in the other one, and without asking for permission, Betty leaned forward and cheekily decided to apply some special coconut styling wax into my thick blue hair, ahhh, what a sweetheart she is. "I like your weird-looking fridge and gas cooker," Said I. "Thanks honey," Betty suddenly became quite chatty. "I love working on my little projects." She took her glasses off, pulled out a tiny pocket mirror, and swiftly put some eye make-up on. "About seventy years ago, I found an old Spitfire plane, it got shot down in the war. I wanted to save the metal y'know, turn it into something new, I got inspired the very next day to make a fridge." Betty opened the Spitfire fridge door, and a light flickered on, inside there was a loaf of bread, some sausages, and a big cheesecake, and at the very back was the Spitfire's actual propeller, spinning slowly, in a calm fashion. Betty installed it specifically to help keep the fridge cool, and also keep the cave warm, she rambled on some more, "I try to get up to London every weekend, Louise. Flying at night is my favourite time to ride, I glide high above the A303, swish past Stone Henge, then I shoot straight up the M3 to London. I love being on the move, it keeps my imagination fresh. Oh dear, look at my fridge, I must go shopping soon." Like a cheeky little kid, Betty reached-in to her weird fridge and boldly poked her finger into the perfect 'yummy-looking' cheesecake, she swiftly scooped a humble sample of fluffy cream onto her index fingertip, and quickly licked it off in one big slurp, then she rambled-on some more. "After making this freaky fridge, I found that I had lots of spare-'Spitfire-metal' left over, so I decided to have a go at making a unique gas cooker," Betty pointed towards the other large shiny vintage object; this gas cooker looked totally smashed up, it most certainly was the only one of its kind. It sported a variety of dents and marks, but it worked perfectly well, it was pretty damn cool actually. Looking around some more, I saw that Betty had a stumpy fat chunky coffee table, cut out from an old English oak tree, and right in the middle of it stood a magnificent colourful Tiffany lamp, it had beautiful stained glassed dragonflies in its pattern, and when she switched it on, all the dragonflies slowly flapped their wings up and down. Oh I say! Hocus-Pocus baby! After seeing all this stuff, I arrived at the foregone conclusion that Betty was bonkers to the bone, but in a good sort of way y'know. I was feeling pretty zonked-out now. I felt comfortable enough to slouch back in the armchair and let my hair down, and by the sound of Betty's sigh, my guess was she felt the same way. I sipped on my pineapple juice while she stuffed a big chunk of tobacco in her old smoking pipe. Her eyes were fixed on me; she had this cheeky smile that kept my eyes fixed on her. Her smile soon grew into a smirk. I had a burning question that I just had to ask now. It's good to ask lots of questions y'know. Don't sit in shy quietness and silently wonder about things, go ahead and ask, just do it! "Betty, you said you found the Spitfire plane about seventy years ago. Well, the thing I don't understand is... you look like you're only about twenty-nine years old, so what's the deal, Sister?" I felt a bit cheeky talking like that, but after our trip over the Atlantic and back, I truly felt it was OK to be up front and chatty, I suddenly wanted to embrace life a bit more. Betty's smile looked exaggerated now, but she was in no rush to answer my question, using a thick dark purple velvet handkerchief she gave her glasses a good wipe-over, then she lit her pipe and started puffing away. She folded her right leg over her left and waited for a long moment before finally speaking up. "I have quite a bit of explaining to do, don't I, Louise? Well, let me start by saying that I absolutely love your pretty little nose, you really do have a gorgeous natural beauty, and I think your blue hair is absolutely-fantastic-bombastic!"

"Why, thank you," I said. Unexpected compliments are always nice to receive. Betty's tone of voice suddenly changed from 'relaxed' to 'more up-tempo'.

"Ok, Louise, make sure you listen very close my dear, the time has now come for me to share the long version with you." I sat up and nodded an affirmative 'Yes.' My pricked-up ears were wide open now, I listened like a cougar in the forest, my mind was finely tuned-in, switched-on to full alert. Betty now had my full, undivided attention. She began to explain things...

"Ok Louise, I'm actually over a hundred years old, but that's not at all important. Like most women, I don't really like discussing my age, so let's skip the trivial chit-chat and get straight to the juicy stuff." Betty sat up.
"Now, I must share this little story with you, you're going to think I'm a total Waco-Fruitcake but… hey-ho. I'll tell you anyway. It's a story about two shooting stars that once cut through the starry skies above, at ridiculous speeds I might add. One star was called 'Roaring Meg' and the other, 'Sonic Sasha.' I want you to know that both these stars were ultra-fast, swishing from universe to universe at the speed of light. But one dark night up in space, they accidentally crashed and smashed into each other, making the biggest explosion you could ever imagine, they lit up the skies like a huge bright silver firework, tons of white glitter sprayed absolutely everywhere. Now, this crash happened just as they were passing over planet Earth, and there's something you ought to know about shooting stars Louise, they fly so fast that it takes them about three hours to slow down to a halt. Now, straight after this ma-hoo-sive collision, both these two shooting beauties bounced off the moon and started making their way down towards planet Earth, they were still travelling at kamikaze speeds, something like 3000 miles per hour. They quickly blasted through the Earth's atmosphere and landed in America, in the hot sunny state of Arizona. This all happened about a hundred thousand

years ago." Betty suddenly paused for a long slow confident puff on her 'Sherlock-Holmes-style' smoking pipe, then she was off again, "Now, when they touched down in Arizona, they hit the ground SO HARD that they ended up ripping right through the solid concrete rocks. They slashed through the Earth's surface like a hot knife cutting through soft butter. This long-winded-crash-landing went on for miles and miles, they ploughed through the earth so intensely that they ended up creating a huge magnificent valley behind them, and these days many tourists go to visit this magnificent place, in these modern times we call this big valley The Grand Canyon."

"Oh, I've heard of that place, it's supposed to be spectacular down there." I said. "Yes, it truly is. The next thing that happened was quite spooky; the impact of the crash knocked these two blazing comets right out of their socks, they were out cold, TKO, completely unconscious, sleeping under a huge pile of bright shiny stardust, and when they woke, a huge transformation had taken place. These cosmic racing electric rocks had now turned from star-form, to human-form. In simple English, they now had human bodies with great powers. My dear Louise, this was the day Roaring Meg became the very first witch ever to exist, and Sonic Sasha became the very first wizard to walk the earth!" I suddenly spat my pineapple juice out, I coughed and giggled, my laughter was getting so out of control.

"Oh Betty, I'm so sorry for laughing, but that bedtime story really does sound like a complete load of camel poo. Do you really expect me to believe a stupid crazy tale like that?" Taking another slow puff on her pipe, Betty replied with an unhurried calmness in her voice, "Well, you've already met Roaring Meg. She was chasing us over the Atlantic Ocean just a few hours ago. I know this story sounds totally nuts, but I said I was going to tell you everything, so please allow your ears to keep absorbing."

Oh, 'Betty the bossy-boots,' I thought to myself. I nodded a sulky yes, then I asked Betty to please continue. She gave me a gracious polite smile, as she delved back into her animated explanations. "Okey, so now I will tell you what happened to the stardust. The huge pile of stardust at the bottom of the new canyon shined magnificently, like glitter under the sun, but it soon lost its spark, and after six hundred seconds, the stardust particles slowly started turning into little bugs, and over the following hour, these ugly little bugs evolved into mini witches, they ended up becoming Roaring Meg's gruesome witch army. Tons of bad energy went into Roaring Meg and her mini witches, while an abundance of good energy went into Sonic Sasha. Meg cursed all the stardust with her dark evil poisonous will, sometimes things just happen like that my love, what can I say?" This story was turning out to be pretty heavy.

A witch army spawned from ugly little bugs, sod that!

Betty had a very simple way of explaining things, she cut through all the penguin-poo in seconds, and I really appreciated this, she rambled on some more,

"Sonic Sasha was a different story altogether. He was already standing up straight, looking like a strong 'man-shaped' wizard. He intuitively knew that the witches were going to create havoc all over the planet, so without wasting a second, he got busy thinking up a solution."

I was curious now, so I asked…"What did Sonic Sasha do, to gain control over Roaring Meg and all the disgusting mini witches, Betty?" Betty smiled,

"Well, being a cosmic space wizard, he had a very fiery imagination, and he soon came up with an excellent idea."

"What was the plan?" I asked. Betty's face suddenly lit up with great joy, she was now telling me all the facts with a tiny glint of pride in her eyes. "At the speed of light, Sonic Sasha flew up to the moon, and using a big fat dose of newly born thunderous wizard magic, he quickly built a beautiful witch library, made from solid white marble stone. He then returned to Arizona disguised as a witch, and successfully persuaded all the mini witches to soar up to the library with him, to learn hundreds of dark evil sinister witchcraft spells. Every single witch immediately followed Sonic Sasha up to the moon, what suckers! Now, this was all a trick of course." Betty winked, as she tapped the side of her pretty forehead with her slender finger.

"Once Sasha had successfully coaxed all the witches into the library, a trap door came crashing down, and they were captured. It was never a library, Sasha made a solid posh-looking marble prison, disguised as a library." I repeated Betty's words, just to make sure I heard her right.

"Hang-on, I just wanna check, Sonic Sasha, dressed in witch-drag, trapped all the mini-witches in a solid marble prison, up on the moon. Is that what you're telling me?"

"Correct-Za-Mundo! That's right my little darling. They all got trapped, except for Roaring Meg, and for a hundred thousand years or so, the old girl's been trying to set them free, but here's the catch, crazy old Roaring Meg needs to find and claim the unique prison key, and that's where you come in, Lou-Bee-Lou, you're in this story" Betty pointed at me. "Why are you pointing right at me?" I asked.

"Because, YOU ARE THE KEY!" I froze up for a second.

"Wait, wait, wait a minute. What do you mean, I am the key?" I was confused now, Betty saw this and immediately started to explain things with more delicate detail.

"Well, you *have* the key inside you, when Sonic Sasha created the marble prison, he knew it would be too simple to just have a normal metal key for opening the prison gates, so he decided, in his vivid spur-of-the-moment imagination, that only a human boomerang-shaped-rib-bone would open the main prison gates." I felt baffled and upset now. "Why did he go for a wacky idea like that?"

"I don't know, I guess back then, boomerang-shaped-human-rib-bones didn't exist." Betty sighed. "But they do now." I felt very nervous and sweaty. "Time-out, time-out! Are you telling me that I'm the only girl in the world with a boomerang-shaped-rib-bone?" "Yes, sugar-bum, that's exactly what I'm saying." Betty went on, "Roaring Meg knows all about this, she knows your funny little rib-bone has a very unique and specific shape, it's the perfect size to work as an effective key, it will open the marble prison gates up there in two seconds, no problemo, please understand that this is exactly what Roaring Meg has been waiting for, so you better get ready sweetheart, cos she's ultra-keen to set those mini-witches free. She'll be bashing on our front door, very soon." I quickly gulped a lump of air the size of a golf ball, I was petrified now. "You must also remember that Roaring Meg is a complete Waco-Nut-Job!" Betty giggled, then she slapped my knee; she was trying to loosen my nerves, but it wasn't working. "Louise, there are three things you need to know about Roaring Meg: One, she's ferociously strong. Two, she doesn't have a conscience, and Three, she will do absolutely anything to get what she wants." Betty leaned in closer, giving me the big green sparkly eyeball, "You must respect her persistence and determination Louise, respecting her willpower and strength will help you stay alive, and hopefully keep you one step ahead."

“She’s one ugly messed-up piece of work, my love. When you harbour anger, along with dark negative thoughts for thousands of years, it does NO favours for your complexion.” Betty suddenly stood up and walked over to the kitchen, “I need a coffee.” She flicked the purple kettle back on and started doing some pilates stretching while waiting for the water to boil. Now, I know I’m just a kid, but I felt like I needed a double whiskey. This was horrible news to receive. My hands shook like autumn leaves clinging to a tree-top in late December. I was full of jumpy jitterbugs now. I trembled all over. I must say, I felt terribly unsettled, I touched my rib cage with my sweaty hand,

and for the first time ever, I noticed that one of my lower ribs, under my right arm, felt bigger than all the others. I guess I had a boomerang rib sitting under my skin. Holy shunka-tunka! I was in big trouble now. I listened to the kettle boil, and soon after, I caught a lovely whiff of the fresh coffee in the air. Betty sat back down in her armchair, sipped on her espresso and immediately burnt her lips. "Mamma Mia, that's way too hot!" She quickly grabbed my pineapple juice and gulped some down. "Ah, that's better." Betty suddenly saw how perturbed I looked, I needed to 'take-five' from all this crazy talk "Hey Louise, the time has come for us to delve deep into some Spitfire cheesecake." That's a great idea. We each had a slice, mama mia, it was super yummy; it had a soft crumbly biscuit base with blueberry jam on top. Betty kept her eyes closed while she ate her slice. The cave was super quiet, but the silence soon got broken by a huge thunderous burp, it wasn't me. Being a lady of strange character, Betty immediately placed her fingertips over her lips and said, "Oops-a-daisy, that sounded like a glitch in the matrix, that didn't just happen, did it?" Betty winked and smiled at me. I giggled and smiled back, then I tucked into the rest of my yummy dessert, our break was nearly over now. All these weird witchy facts were pretty hard to take in, I had way too much fear in my tummy. Betty now looked ready to jump back-into her cool rambling chatter-box mode.

"I want you to know that, Sonic Sasha the great wizard was my father, but he died, sadly, from a very strong magic overdose, back in 1973. He pretty much vanished into thin air, and nobody has seen him since." Betty paused for a long moment, and for a few dragging seconds I saw a fleeting glimmer of sadness flicker through her eyes, acting fast she quickly blinked the sadness away and continued with my education, "Now you can understand, and see why Roaring Meg saved you from the swimming pool accident, back when you were around six years old."

"What! Hang on, how the hell do you know about that?"

Betty slid her bum over to the edge of her chair and calmly whispered into my ear.

"Well, my little angel, some people know a lot about little things, but the key to living a good interesting life is to know a little about a lot of things." She laughed out loud.

"Meg knew about your rib back then, and so did I, but it was best that I stayed out of the picture – till now of course. Meg has patiently been waiting for your rib to grow just that little bit extra, and now her window of opportunity has finally arrived, she plans to shamelessly rip into your chest like a wild Bengal Tiger, and steal your rib away. You just gotta hang tough honey, you will naturally keep growing into a young beautiful woman, and of course your boomerang rib will keep growing too. Soon, it will be too big for Meg to use as a key. I reckon that old hag will be coming here real soon though, we just need to make sure we're ready for her, she's one crazy old junk-yard mongrel, a real mad-dog, you must remember this, gotta respect her malicious determination, respect her dark undying willpower, and persevering spirit." There was an unflinching conviction in Betty's serious voice.

"Just remember that… more than anything in this world, Meg wants to set those witches free, she's totally blind-addicted to power, she's a sick-crooked-control-freak, with a massive ego, she wants to rule this whole planet! It sounds crazy but it's true, that wicked witch wants to take over the whole human race by brainwashing the minds of millions, she wants to turn people into zombie-slaves and fill them with sheepish self-doubt. Some people are so twisted, old Meg is absolutely barking! Remember, she has no conscience." Betty was disgusted by Roaring Meg's ugly plans of selfish world domination. I listened to my guardian angel go on, all the energy coming out of Betty's heart was pure raw emotion, she meant every word. I felt lucky to be with her, she was my strength. She suddenly switched her old record player on and blasted-out a tune called, 'Judy In Disguise.' She hopped and danced around the cave like a happy hippy, she forced me to get up and boogie too, I felt very silly, but I can't deny that all the twisting and groovin helped me forget about the dark stuff, for a few minutes anyway.

CHAPTER 7

HERE WE GO AGAIN

When the song finished, Betty played another tune called 'Wooly Bully.' I danced like crazy, then I sat back in my chair and tried my best to digest all the info she had told me; it wasn't easy. It's not every day you find out that some crazy witch wants to catch you, rip your chest open and take one of your ribs away. There was an overflow of anxious energy running through my veins, a wild river of miscellaneous thoughts creating unpleasant images in my head, it felt like I had a weird David Lynch movie playing in my brain, and I couldn't switch it off. I tried to relax but it felt like mission impossible. Silence filled the cave, but my mind was louder than a discotheque. That all suddenly changed however, when I heard a creaking noise come from behind the cave walls, it sounded like a deep rumble of hunger, festering down in the pit of a dragon's belly, maybe it was an earthquake tremor? "Oh dear, it looks like Meg has already found us. See Louise, I told you, she's one ultra-determined monster!" "Holy crackers with cream. That was quick!" Betty grabbed my hand and quickly took me into the cave next door, it was pitch black, we suddenly heard a second rumble, Betty sighed as she spoke up. "My goodness, Meg sure is one crazy old pig." She slapped the cave walls with passion, making silly animal sounds, she sounded like a wild happy monkey who'd won the lottery.

"Hoo-Hoo-Hoo! We're over here, rat face." Betty couldn't give a damn about Meg, she was pretty much carefree about everything. She quickly clapped her hands twice, like a busy bistro head waitress, and a light suddenly came on. "Right, Louise, here's the current situation. I've got this other project I've been working on for two years, and due to our present circumstances, I think NOW would be a good time for us to give it a test run. What d'ya say?"

"Absolutely yes!" I said this with zero hesitation.

"I just hope your two year project gets us out of here fast!"

"Oh yes, it will certainly do that." There was a relaxed confidence in Betty's voice, it was so nice to hear, it gave me some unexpected comfort in the midst of all this madness. We were standing in front of a large mystery object now, it sat under an old canvas cover, so without wasting another second, we quickly pulled the cover off together. "Mama-Shoop-Shoop! Oh I say, what have we got here then?" I asked. At first glimpse, this 'thing' looked like a strange piece of abstract art, but it turned out to be something far more eccentric than that. It was a one of a kind, custom-made, sixty-six-valve, twin-turbo, low-riding sports car, made completely from second-hand chrome washing machine parts – a 'Betty-Boo-Speciality.'

"Check it out, Lou-bee-Lou. Under the hood we've got huge amounts of horse-power, buffalo-power, tiger-power, lion-power, any power you want, I got it right here, kid."

I know this is a little off-topic, but I love the smell of horses. Anyway, my danger-lovin guardian angel smiled and said, "Burt Munro would have loved this little beauty." Betty built the whole vehicle from scratch: the wheels were old washing machine drums, the steering wheel was an old washing machine door, the beefy engine was made from ten different washing machine motors – it was ridiculously powerful. The only things that didn't come from washing machine were the tires and the seats. It had two old sports car bucket seats from an old Porsche, and a big old tatty Chesterfield oxblood leather sofa in the back. Quickly checking the fuel gauge, Betty noticed that the tank was completely empty, now reaching down and ripping open a big box of washing powder, she proceeded to pour the whole lot in the tank. "What are you doing?" I asked. "I need to fill her up," she said. I couldn't believe my eyes. "You mean to tell me that this car runs on washing powder? Is that right? Are you serious?"

"Yes, of course," said Betty. As soon as the tank was full, we both jumped-in and put our seat-belts on, Betty started to rub her legs up and down like a happy kid who was about ready to open all her Christmas presents. She gave me a slow strong wink. "Yaba-Ding-Doo! I'm so looking forward to this, Kato." She was rubbing her hands together now, like a Las Vegas gambler hoping to throw a lucky number seven with her dice. Funnily enough, she had some fluffy dice hanging from the rear view mirror. "I call this baby, The Spinner," Betty slapped my leg with frivolous joy, she was terribly excited about giving this cool vehicle its 'make or break' test run; the spinner was a most peculiar invention. Betty started her up on the first try, she smugly smirked at me with some 'smarty-pants' pride in her eyes. The cool car sounded like a beefy Harley Davidson chopper, it wobbled about like crazy, after sixty seconds the engine suddenly changed its tune, it started making lots of weird high-pitched-dandy-popping sounds now, no smoke blew from the exhaust pipe, just foam mixed with bubbles. We suddenly felt the cave-walls vibrate again, Meg was close by now, I picked-up her low seedy vibrations in the air, dark-evil-poisonous-wilful-witch-rage, yikes! It was a morbid yukky feeling. The spinner suddenly jolted forward a couple of feet, Betty smiled and shouted at the top of her voice, "Hold on to your eggs and apples, Kemosabe, we might end up in Neverland after this one. Make some new space in your heart, cos it's about to get blasted with pure JOY-RIDE-FEVER!" She pushed her foot flat down on the accelerator pedal, and the spinner shot-off like a giant chrome killer pinball! SCHOOOOOM! "Whooooo-hooooooo! Nice one Betty" I shouted."Ha-Ha! Let the good times roll baby!" The force of the acceleration pushed both our heads right back against our retro bucket seats. Here we go again, ha! We drove up a dark winding tunnel that led out to a secret doorway, the spinner came blasting out onto Portobello Road, London W11. Zooming past the Happy Donut shop, Betty cheekily grabbed a raspberry Jam striker, she took one bite and gave the rest to me, we headed south now. We had to get out of the area fast, but it wasn't going to be easy, the spinner was slipping and sliding all over the place, its engine was too damn powerful; it wheel-spinned like we were driving on a thin icy lake, Betty laughed out loud while she crashed into many parked cars, next up we heard a huge crashing noise come from behind us, I looked around to check it out, oh my lord, I saw another strange vehicle come up from under the ground. It smashed through the pavement in a totally disgraceful manner. It was Meg of course, she was driving some kind of advanced high-speed tank, a weird ugly concrete-crusher. As soon as I saw her red eyes, my body began to shiver. I tried so hard to turn my nervous feelings into excitement, but it wasn't easy, the fear was crazy, I'm proud to say that I didn't wet my knickers this time. Meg followed us all the way up Portobello Road, this is a one-way street, and we were both going up it the wrong way; the spinner zig-zagged all over the place. I shouted out to all the people walking along both sides of the street, "Gang way! Gang way! We're coming through!" To avoid getting crushed, people jumped up onto parked cars and dived into shop doorways. Meg's reckless driving was just as terrible, she couldn't drive straight to save her life, but she was gaining on us, her robust concrete-crusher was surprisingly fast. As we turned a sharp corner, Betty suddenly noticed a fat scruffy looking couple sitting at the bus stop, they were sipping coffees and stuffing jam doughnuts down their throats. So, faster than a cheetah, Betty stopped the car, ran over, picked them up, and threw them onto the backseat sofa. I had no idea what she was up to. "Betty, what are you doing?" I shouted. "Trust me," that was all she said. Meg was heading straight for us now, she wanted to ram us down, no doubt about it, Betty moved ever so quick, she got back behind the wheel and quickly did naught to sixty in three seconds flat, this put us back out in front for a while, she turned to the chubby folks and spoke up, "Good morning Sir. Good morning Madam. Me and my wild-little-blue-haired-sidekick-racer here are offering free joy-rides today, we heard on the news that all the bus drivers have gone home to meditate, so please just sit back, relax, and let us take you to your chosen destination. Hold on to your knickers, and pray we don't crash." Betty suddenly punched her fist right up into the sky, and shouted wildly with sheer delight, "Yeeeee-Haaaaaaa! IT'S PARTY TIME BABY!" She behaved like a wild crazy cowgirl super fan, cheering at a Taylor Swift concert. I was struggling big-time now, trying so hard to hold my laughter in,

I turned around to politely welcome the chubby couple on board, but when I saw the stunned look on their faces, I couldn't help but giggle, the poor souls were in a state of complete shock and panic, but they still managed to carry on scoffing their doughnuts, oink-oink. They were funny to watch, they spilt most of their cappuccinos on their laps, they looked like two grizzly bears stuck inside a rollercoaster car, they clung on to that chesterfield sofa like a couple of slobs refusing to go to bed, they had big fat sausage fingers. After scoffing down the last mouthful of his strawberry jam doughnut, the fat man quickly put his hands together and started to pray, we turned a sharp corner next, and losing her balance, the nervous fat woman fell and squeezed *her* doughnut so hard that all the jam squirted out, it went straight into the fat man's ear. I had to quickly pretend to cough as a way of covering up my laughter, Betty was giggling too. I was so impressed with her sharp genius idea though, her quick thinking paid off terribly well. Our new backseat passengers turned out to be the perfect solution for our car troubles, their combined 'piano-like' body weight held the spinner down beautifully. It stuck to the road like a heavy go-kart now – no more slipping and sliding out of control. Nice one Betty, you Bonsai beach babe! We were dashing through London pretty fast now, but we still had our work cut out, the wild witchy super-freak was still hot on our heels. Oh-by-Jingo, looking in the side-view mirror I saw the concrete-crusher lash out like a mad bulldozer, in thirty seconds flat it trampled over and completely demolished ten vespa motorbikes, a beautiful metallic navy blue 1966 Porsche, and a sweet cherry red 1965 Ferrari Dino, oh my goodness, Meg was breaking hearts all over town. The chubby couple kindly leaned into the corners now, we took a few sharp lefts followed by some razor-blade rights, but Meg wasn't lettin up, no way, she had a one-track mind. We smashed through some black iron gates and steamed our way into Hyde Park. The chubsters clung onto each other now, the big woman yelled out, "Where are the flippin seat-belts!?" She looked like Mama Cass, from the 'Mamas and Papas,' that's an old sixties pop band. Betty replied,

"There aren't any, you just have to hold on tight, Cookie!"

"Oh I say, I quite fancy a cookie," said the chubby hubby.

We rushed over to Kensington Gardens, racing like a wild chicken being chased by a crazy fox. Betty was right, Meg is ridiculously determined. Like two stunt drivers, we slid back out onto the main road and zoomed past the Royal Albert Hall in a flash. Betty pointed to a big poster, "No way! Hey check it out Louise, the Rolling Stones are doing a gig tonight, maybe we can pop by later." Soon after that we were speeding outside Buckingham Palace. Out by the front gates we wheel-spinned around that posh gold angel statue at least twenty times. Big bold donut skids. Therewere skid-marks left all over the road, and probably a few more in the fat man's underpants. This was the first time I got a clear view of Meg's revolting face. She looked pretty rough y'know, I saw those red eyes shining through a black pair of biker's goggles, her strange thorny hair looked like dead bramble, her will-power was so impressive. She snarled like a crazy mongoose with rabies, her yellow stubby pirate teeth looked awful, and her gums were jet black, then, very unexpectedly, her teeth popped-out, ah man! They were dentures! For a second I thought a dirty old frog had just escaped her gob. Meg skilfully caught her teeth and quickly shoved them back in, this probably wasn't the first time she did this, my o my. She had big bushy nose hair and red warts all over her face, the long whiskers sprouting from her man-shaped-chin looked like broken violin strings. She had two massive blobs of foamy saliva-string hanging out the side of her mouth. I couldn't imagine any man ever wanting to French kiss her, I'd rather French kiss a donkey. Betty was getting a lot of enjoyment from this chase; her 'adrenaline-junkie-persona' was getting a good fix. Still spinning wildly, she switched the radio on and cranked the volume right up. "Oh, I love this song!" She said. It was 'Sweet Home Alabama' by Lynyrd Skynyrd. The fat man in the back spoke up, "Hey, turn it up some more, this is my favourite band in the whole world, I absolutely love these guys!" I think he was telling the truth y'know, he sang with great passion, and he knew every single word. Betty was very impressed, she turned around to give Mr Chubby a quick high-five, and we all suddenly noticed how Mrs Chubby was now using her iphone to take pictures of Buckingham Palace, Betty spoke up in her silly posh hostess voice,

"Let's take the scenic route round the back, my sweet little darlings. I'm sure we can snap some pretty shots of the royal gardens." The chubby man wanted to go to the nearest drive-thru, to murder a double cheeseburger, but there was no time for pit-stops, we were still being chased. Betty smashed the spinner right through the main gates of Buckingham Palace, and quickly sped across the courtyard, Meg followed close behind. We shot past the butler's quarters and quickly busted through a small side-door that led straight to the glorious royal back gardens, we just missed an old bearded gardener, he dived out of the way and landed in some rose bushes. Holy Smoke, both our vehicles made such a mess, crazy Meg ripped through everything, she drove like a blind pensioner hand-cuffed to the wheel of a runaway bumper car, taking big chunks of concrete out of the palace walls, she completely flattened a beautiful garden shed, she was such a bad driver, maybe she was drunk? We tore the back lawn up something terrible. Meg annihilated four lovely water fountains, while Betty demolished five beautiful marble statues. The chubby duo in the back were taking many pictures now, snapping away like crazy, acting like the paparazzi, maybe they were planning to sell their photos to 'HELLO' magazine? The next thing that happened took all of us by surprise, especially me. Roaring Meg grabbed her black surfboard from the backseat, and faster than a wasp, she flew over to the spinner, swooped down, and yanked me right out of my seat. Holy-sheep-shish-kebab, she moved so fast! "Louise!" Shouted Betty. I was filled with terror. Meg had a mighty strong grip on me. She picked me up like an eagle, I was locked-in under her arm, squeezed tightly into her body; her cold bony hands actually looked like eagle claws. Meg laughed aggressively as we flew off together on that speeding surfboard, she was one mean old witch. I guess she was unhappy with the grip she had, cos she let me go, flipped me round, and caught my leg in mid-flight. I was hanging upside down now, all the blood went rushing to my head, heaven help me, this upside down predicament instantly made me feel giddy, nauseous and dizzy. I was so damn scared. Driving back out onto the main road Betty tried her best to keep up with us, but she had no chance, Meg and I were already flying halfway off into the distance. I was praying hard now, holy father help me, I'd never felt fear like this before. I was finding it hard to breathe, I think I was on the verge of blacking out. "Hang on Louise! Hang tough my love! Don't give up! I will find you!" Betty was livid. All this upside-down dangling around monkey business kind of made me feel like blowing some chunks, I was slipping in and out of consciousness, my mind was all over the place, being held the wrong way up felt so unnatural, I felt sick, this experience got me thinking about bats for a second, why the hell do they sleep upside down? I guess Batman knows the answer to that. Meg's flying surfboard suddenly picked up more speed, I just about managed to give Betty a quick thumbs-up, then I fainted. I was in a deep dark sticky pickle now, felt like I was stuck in the middle of a morbid gloomy nightmare. I had no idea where she was taking me; it wasn't Disneyland, I knew that much. Betty quickly made her way back to Portobello Road, dropping the chubby couple off at Ladbroke Grove tube station, she gave a fiver to Mr chubby, to buy a couple of cheeseburgers, and five pounds to Mama Cass, to buy some fresh doughnuts from the Sainsbury's store under the bridge. Arriving back at her laundromat, Betty wasted no time at all, she parked the spinner back down in the secret hideout cave, knocked back a cold cup of coffee, quickly put some fresh lip-stick on, grabbed her jet powered rocket ironing board, and got ready to make a sharp exit, but just before taking off, she went up to her laundromat to open the shop for business, she had six customers waiting outside, all of them were holding big bags full of dirty washing.

Betty let them in, switched the radio on, quickly found a good sunny spot for her dragon-fire daffodil, pushed her pink goggles down over her face, zipped her red puffer jacket up, threw her trusty ironing board down to the ground, and blasted off into the sky.

Yes!

Go Betty!

Go-Girl!

Go-Go-Go-Girl!

Please come and find me!

I swear, that girl has the heart and soul of a true champion legend. Her spirit was unbreakable, her cheeky personality reminded me a little bit of Muhammad Ali. She was a true fighter, a never-giver-upper.

You've got to be a true fighter in this crazy old world, otherwise people will just walk all over you.

I think it's good to be cheeky too.

Make some people smile along the way, and they will like you.

There you go, some nice free advice for you to suck on.

The next chapter coming up is a bit of a rough ride.

That brutal witch almost killed me….

Almost.

CHAPTER 8

THE TOUGHEST DAY OF MY LIFE

Betty's mission was simple: she needed to find me before Meg yanked my rib out, but things didn't look good. I was already tied up in her witch cave somewhere on the outskirts of North London. I say 'witch cave,' but in truth, it was more like a dark deserted warehouse. Betty knew how to find me; it was a 'mind over matter' situation. She flew herself way up high to a zenith position in the sky, and there she meditated for a while, keeping completely still, she sat 'legs-crossed' on her hovering Ironing board, looking like a pretty little buddhist. Betty's senses were ultra-sharp, breathing deep and slow she relaxed herself into a peaceful vibration, this automatically put her on a higher frequency level. In this 'zen-like' state, Betty was now able to hear my voice and pick up my energy, she's a pretty talented individual you know; she *is* the daughter of a wizard after all, just don't mention her age. Ha-ha.

This truly was the toughest day of my life. Meg's warehouse was a cold, damp, grotesque, shabby-hide-out-hole, a huge open freezing cold space, it was full of dead rats, I saw a pile of them in the corner, some were half eaten, they stunk! The whole place was a tip. This was the day Meg snatched my rib away, in the most disgusting fashion, strapping me down to an old wooden bench she cut me wide open, what a sick, twisted, messed up loser. Using a blunt rusty old dagger, she cut into me and proceeded to yank my little boomerang-rib straight from my chest. Sweet lord, it hurt so much! Don't worry, it didn't kill me; I made it through, didn't I? Of course I did. I'm here telling you my story now, but it was still a very tough experience, I was far too close to death, I tell ya.

While performing this tragic sin, Meg laughed out loud like a crazy old goofy goblin girl, she didn't behave like a responsible doctor, far from it, she committed this terrible act of thievery like an obsessed cave woman, panting and dribbling all over me like a mad demented blood-thirsty wolf-hound, she had no remorse at all, she's such a freak.

"Yes! Yes! I have the key. I have the key! At last!"

This was a glorious, victorious moment for Meg. Holding my rib up high, she danced around the warehouse like an obsessed evil gipsy spirit, jumping about like that dopey tiger from Winnie the Pooh. Leaping as high as she could, she accidentally head-butted and smashed a light bulb above her, and without any warning, she found herself on the receiving end of some hardcore powerful electric shocks. The crazy old rat jittered about up there for a good ten seconds, all the other lights flickered on and off. Her hard-head must've smashed through to a thick 'live' wire cable, two seconds later her dentures fell out, and all the other bulbs exploded. She crashed back down to the dark dirty floor like a wing-less she-devil falling from the sky. I couldn't see much now that the lights were off, but I heard a thud that was followed by a huge wet fart, after that I heard lots of grumpy growling grovelling groans, Meg moaned away like an old wincing werewolf who'd just been hit by a car, she constantly rolled about on the wet concrete floor. Her big fart was followed by a tiny bubble-pop fart, I'm sure I heard a small witchy giggle after that, two seconds later she was back on her feet, bouncing and dancing around again. Her dark joy seemed to push all the daylight away, it was weird; it felt like the whole universe had turned grey and grim in a heartbeat, there was only a faint dim orange flickering light flashing through the window now, it must have been an old faulty street lamp outside. Behaving like she'd just won the world cup, Meg held her trophy (my rib) up high for the world to see. In the limited shadowy light, I saw her knock back a pint glass that was full to the rim with Jack Daniels whiskey, she didn't drink it, she just gargled the strong spirit for a while, she spat every drop back into the glass, this salivary pint of brown whiskey now had cockroaches swimming in it, man, this witch was revolting. Meg suddenly knelt down to pick her dentures up, she purposely dropped them in her pint, I watched her disgusting false teeth slowly knock the drowning cockroaches down to the bottom of the glass, sweet heavens above, this rough old girl was vile.

Still tied to the old wooden bench, I looked down and saw that I was bleeding quite bad, I was in a state of high-adrenaline-shock, and disbelief. Meg had a little limp now, walking towards me she offered the pint glass up to my face, "Fancy a drink, love?" I closed my eyes tightly and nodded a quick passionate 'NO' – this disgusting witch was shameless. She started laughing and dancing and spinning around like a mentally disturbed drunk ballerina, she raised her glass high, and with a toothless smile she looked straight into my eyes and said, "To your rib, little girl. Bottoms up!" She downed all the whiskey, swallowed all the cockroaches, and slipped her dentures back in her mouth, all in one big swooping gulp. This solo toast was followed by a huge belch that echoed all around the dark shabby warehouse. The belch made some of the rats jump. This was the day I realised just how horrible Meg truly is, but I must admit, the cool way she put those dentures back in was a pretty smooth party trick. Everything in my mind started to make sense, y'know. I finally understood why she saved me from that freezing cold swimming pool, back in Devon, when I was just five and three quarters. It was all about this moment; it was all about getting her hands on my bloody boomerang rib. I just don't know what to say about that, some people are so messed-up, they act like selfish twats and forget how to think about other people. Selfishness is a terrible curse.

Holy hot potatoes, I thought this was the end of the line for me. Meg left me lying in a puddle of my own blood. I'm sorry to tell you this; I know it's not a pretty picture, my strength and spirit rested on thin ice. I can honestly say, from the bottom of my heart, that this was the toughest day of my life. That gipsy pig placed my rib in her mouth, bit down on it like a wild dog, and laughed passionately. She had all the characteristics of a self-centred psycho. Hopping back on her black surfboard she started to sing, 'Fly me to the Moon,' and WHOOOOSH! Out the door she flew. I looked out the window and saw her disappear-off into the cloudy skies above. It was pretty obvious where she was going. So there I was, left to die on that shabby old wooden bench, my heart and soul felt crushed, my temperature had dropped immensely, I'd lost so much blood, I was absolutely freezing, shivering like a little lamb left out in the snow. "Betty," I murmured. I kept whispering her name over and over. "Betty, please come find me, please save me." I said this about two hundred times, for the next twenty minutes; I felt beaten-up and defeated. But then, finally, my prayer was answered. My wild eccentric supersonic surrogate auntie arrived, in the most glorious fashion. The way she broke-in was spectacular, the only thing missing was a red superman cape flapping behind her. Keeping perfect balance on her jet-powered rocket ironing board, Betty smashed through the big warehouse windows, broken glass flew everywhere.

Yes! I was running low on time, I was dying man! No doubt about it. I kept seeing this bright white light shining out in front of me. It was an angel, coming to collect me, I heard all these heavenly voices, then I heard Betty's voice, she was shouting out as loud as she could.

"Go away!" She said to the angel.

"Louise has her whole life in front of her. Come back another time, when she's ninety-seven years old!"

The bright light graciously faded away.

"Hang in there, Louise," said Betty.

"Let the rescue commence!" She announced, with a cheeky tone in her voice. Thank God for Betty. She quickly wrapped me up in her big red ski jacket and flew me out of there. I had no idea where we were going now. Everything in my mind was fuzzy. I vaguely remember Betty saying something about visiting a graveyard.

"You need purple magic," she said. Betty did everything in her power to keep me alive, bless her soul. Purple magic is something that lived inside Sonic Sasha's heart, it's strong potent stuff. Betty knew that purple magic was the only kind of cosmic medicine that could bring me back, and she knew exactly where we could find some, we headed over to the cemetery by Swain's Lane, up in Highgate. It was a gamble, but hopefully we'd get lucky. Sonic Sasha used purple magic to create the amazing marble prison, up on the moon.

create the amazing marble prison, up on the moon. Purple magic is the opposite of black magic; purple magic has many healing properties, it's bold rich stuff, it's pretty awesome gear to be honest. It could make a dead forest rich and green again. I never knew this but once a year, every Christmas, Betty went to visit her dad's grave in Highgate Cemetery, just to wish his spirit a Merry Christmas. Well, this was the exact place she took me. On arrival, I thought she was going to bury me right next to her old man. I had no idea what she was up to. The fire in my heart was dying out, I knew that much. As soon as we landed, Betty started digging deep into the earth. Her plan was to try and find some of her late father's bones, she believed her dad's wizard-bones just might have some purple magic sleeping deep inside, way down in the marrow. Betty was fully aware that her dad disappeared from a magic overdose, and she knew full-well that there was only a slim chance of finding something under his gravestone. No coffin was buried at his funeral, but Sonic Sasha was a crafty old bugger, a shrewd dude full of mystical secrets, he thought like a fox who knew how to play blackjack and win every time. Knowing all about her father's savvy nature and forward-thinking attitude, Betty believed fervently, that he just might have left something buried at his tombstone, something that might help us get out of the terrible jam we were in. My back was up against the wall, big time baby! It was late in the morning, and I was dying right there on the cold ground. Now, we all know that Betty ain't no quitter, no sir-ree, far from it. She wasn't going to just let me lie back, turn up my toes and bite the dust - oh no, that wasn't her style, and I certainly wasn't ready to throw the towel in. I wanted to live, more than ever! Betty moved at tip-top speed, digging crazy like a caffeine-addicted mole. I opened my eyes and suddenly saw that bright white light again - sweet kittens in mittens, here we go again. I think it was a pure spirit y'know, a sacred heavenly angel.

"No!" shouted Betty. "It's not her time! Go away, angel girl. Louise is staying right here, with me!" The holy light faded away again. Holy hotdogs, Betty sure could be one bossy babe when she wanted to, it was all passion I guess.

"Keep strong, Louise!" She dug awfully fast, but found nothing in the earth - no bones, no coffin, not a thing. Being stuck in this fatal condition was no fun at all, believe me, my only goal at the time was to keep breathing, but even that suddenly became a steep challenge, lots of cold earth kept landing on my face and falling into my mouth, making me cough and choke. Betty was flicking loose soil all over the place. She dug like a crazy old Jack Russell, not giving a hoot about where all the mud might be landing. It didn't bother me too much, it helped me stay awake to be honest, my spirit was being tested today. I felt like a wounded gazelle out in Africa. I started thinking about my folks, wondering where they might be, maybe one of them died, I don't know. All Betty's constant digging was about to pay off, she suddenly hit something - yes! The sound was like a low-pitched thud, and seconds later, she pulled out an old wooden shoebox, excellent! A warm feeling of hope suddenly filled the air. Quickly opening the box Betty found two items inside: a letter and a rib - what a sweet result. The rib had a strong purple glow to it; it must have belonged to Sasha. "Hold this," said Betty, placing the rib in my hand. Now, as soon as I touched that little gem, I immediately felt stronger inside; I knew I was absorbing some kind of unique healing energy. Whatever it was, it brought me back. Betty quickly read the letter. This is what it said: 'To my darling daughter, Betty. This is your father, Sonic Sasha. Hey beautiful, how are you? I have some good news for you - I'm still alive! I live out in a remote spot, high up in the Italian mountains. I had a feeling that, one day, someone might be needing one of my ribs, so I decided to leave one in the cemetery. It has a great deal of purple magic inside. It will help the poor soul who needs it, no doubt. Betty, I love you with all my heart, and I really want to see you soon, please come visit me. I will explain many things to you, in great detail, when I see you. I still think about you all the time sugar-puff, with everlasting love, your father, Sonic Sasha x' Wow! This letter filled Betty's heart up with joy and fresh excitement, her sparkling green eyes turned the teary taps on, she was going to see her dad again – how cool is that? This blew her mind. She quickly wiped her eyes and brought all her attention back to me. "Righty-ho, little girl, let's get you back into tip-top form."

There was a new zest in Betty's voice. She gently took her father's rib from my hand and placed it on top of my open wound. Keeping serenely still she watched over me like Florence Nightingale, I took a deep breath as the rib suddenly cranked its magic up; it glowed intensely, like it was waking up. I saw this with my own eyes. It gave off a wonderful pinkish/ purple light, it crackled like kindling wood in a log fire, then it suddenly turned a dark fiery orange colour. Betty smiled kindly as she patiently watched the marvellous purple magic go to work on me. This rib knew exactly what to do; it behaved like an advanced conscious living intelligence. It firmly push itself into my wound, changing shape as it went in. It hurt like hell, but only for ten seconds, on the eleventh second all the pain disappeared, phew-wee! Sasha's rib was brimming with positive energy now. It automatically installed itself into my rib cage, positioning itself exactly where my boomerang rib once sat; and it moved in forever, it's still inside me now, sitting comfortably. I was fixed and healed in ninety five seconds, holy smoking flip flops! Purple magic sure is a wondrous thing. IT ROCKS! Betty gently scooped her hand around the back of my neck and slowly encouraged me to tilt my head up. I helped myself up on to my elbows and gazed down at my open wound. I watched with wonder, as my body speedily knitted new skin over my open chest - it was amazing. I was so impressed. The purple magic soon found it's way into my flesh and bones, like a river of joy it flowed all around my bloodstream, I could even taste it in my mouth, it was a warm cinnamon taste mixed with brown sugar and yummy honey, I could get used to this. Three minutes went by and I was now standing up straight, feeling like a champion. I felt great, I quickly gave the green-eyed-wonder-woman the biggest hug I could manage, "Thank you, Betty," That's all I could say, I was so grateful!

"Thank you, thank you, thank you so much!" Betty was the coolest cat ever. "Breathe deep, girl," that was all she said. I suddenly began to really cherish being alive. A feeling of calm grace suddenly came right up from my toes, filling my whole body. Betty pulled her father's letter out and showed it to me. I noticed his Italian address was scribbled on the back. "Well spotted," she said. Betty suddenly paused for a long moment, I think she was reflecting on my recent dilemma, she gave me that rich abundant unflinching stare again, in her imagination, I think she was trying to put herself in my shoes, just for the last two hours of my life, y'know. "Sweet fuzz nuts, that trip must have been quite a traumatic ride for you, Louise."

"Yes ma'am, it sure was, very intense indeed. Let's do it again, are you free tomorrow?" I laughed and winked, of course I was joking. Betty had an idea now, I saw the light change in her big green 'exploding-firework' eyes. "Hey! Let's go grab a milkshake!" She smiled like she was ten years old. "We've no time to waste. I know a great milkshake bar just up the road." Betty slapped my bum before she jumped back on her rocket flying board, she was filled with zeal, and I was filled with sharper senses, this new magic inside felt like an upgrade from mother nature.

"Come on Cookie face, let's go!" So off we went. I got myself a vanilla ice cream shake filled with freshly chopped strawberries. Betty's shake had crushed coconut biscuits mixed with Belgian chocolate ice cream, yum. She drank hers way too fast; she was ultra keen to get out to Italy, to see her dad, this was completely understandable. Keeping a cool balance on her ironing board, Betty stood in a power stance, with both hands on her hips; she looked like a true superhero now. Well, she WAS a true superhero to me. In the last 24 hours she saved my life twice, and thought nothing of it, it was just another day at the office for her. "Right, it's time we head over to Italia. Are you ready to Rock and Roll some more, my tough little side-kick-wild-cat?" I smiled and nodded, and daring to stare right into Betty's face, I cheekily meowed an enthusiastic yes, then I went back to

sucking hard on my milkshake straw.
"Good-O," she said "Hop back on the board my little ladybird, come along now, it's time for us to move our groove along." I finished my shake and did just that. We had to be quick because Roaring Meg was no doubt already up on the moon, tinkering about with my boomerang rib, slowly figuring out how to open the marble prison gates. We quickly zoomed back up into the cold grey sky, and put shabby old London behind us.
"Italia, Italia, here we come bambina," Betty was pumped with passion now, she loves her dad just like Nancy loves Frank Sinatra. My old man loves Frank Sinatra's music.
This was my first trip to Italy, Bella Bella Bella!
I hope we get to eat some fresh lasagne, and maybe enjoy some spaghetti bolognese.
I just love pasta. I love Betty too.
All these strange happenings were very extraordinary, but deep down inside, I was loving every minute of it. By this time I just decided to go with the flow, this was so much better than going to school. Come to think of it, I'm quite pleased our old washing machine blew up!
That weird fiasco changed my life for the better.
Off we flew to Italy, with cold milkshakes in our tummies, and no passports in our back-pockets. Ha-ha!

CHAPTER 9

LUNCH IN THE MOUNTAINS

Our flight to Italy was fantastic. Gliding and weaving through the craggy mountain landscape was breath-taking; everything was fresh, bright and glorious. It felt really good riding the rocket ironing board with nobody chasing us. I wasn't exactly sure which part of Italy we were in, I think it was the Dolomites, all the surroundings were gorgeous. There were snow-capped mountains in the distance, and all the valleys below had big lakes in them, and when the sun hit their surface, they shined like huge majestic puddles of pure liquid silver. The natural beauty of this environment stood out magnificently - the rich scent of the pine trees, the birds singing, the sound of the mountain streams, it felt like paradise, it was a great place for a wizard to go into exile. This just goes to show that Sasha has exceptional taste. Arriving at his pad, I became super excited to meet him, but I decided to sit back and play it cool. I knew this was a big deal for Betty, seeing her papa for the first time in years was obviously going to be emotional, for both parties. Sasha had his own little business - it was a one-stop-road-side-coffee-shop, set up in an old limestone mountainside house, it sat all alone by a rocky road, this old trail was mainly used by Italian lorry drivers and summertime tourists, taking the scenic route off the beaten track. It was a pretty little café, the whole front wall and main entrance was completely covered by an overgrowth of winter jasmine, mixed with wisteria; it looked lovely. Leaping off the rocket board, I remember seeing lots of pretty little birds hanging out by the café's front door, all just waiting to be fed. Sasha gave them ripped-up broken bits of freshly baked bread every morning. One of these little guys had a red chest and a funny little bomber hat, he looked very familiar. Yes, it was the same dude I met years before, the Brighton bird flying alongside Dad's red VW beetle, back when I was just a toddler, ha-ha, that's so crazy.

The energy outside suddenly increased when the cool wizard graced us with his presence. Sonic Sasha came walking out the front door singing 'Bohemian Rhapsody' at the top of his voice. He had a little bread basket in his hand, but when he saw Betty, he dropped everything and shouted her name out-loud, with all his heart.

"BETTEEEEEEEEEEEEEEEEE," he roared.

His 'lion-like' voice echoed all around the mountains.

This turned out to be a very emotional reunion for both these souls. They cried, hugged and sobbed all over each other; it was quite sweet really. I then noticed something strange about Sasha's tears; they behaved in a freaky topsy-turvy fashion. Instead of rolling down the cheeks, they ran up his face. I don't know if this happens with all wizards, but it certainly did with Sasha, his aura seemed to make Betty's tears roll up too.

Many tears dashed up to the top of their heads and quickly seeped back into their brains, creating all kinds of cosmic thoughts I suppose. Wizard tears prevent hair from turning grey, which is pretty awesome when you think about it. Betty's tears speedily rolled around in tiny circles on her forehead, before slipping back up into the pink fuzz, he-he.

Betty truly had no idea that Sasha had been living out in the Italian sticks for all these years; she really thought her father was dead, and Sasha felt terrible about this, but what could he do? This was the only way he could stay one step ahead of Roaring Meg. She wanted to kill Sasha so badly, for trapping her witch army, all those years ago, she's filled with poisonous resentment, and mental venom. When the tears finally stopped rolling-up, and the cosmic father and daughter finally stopped hugging, Sasha turned and kneeled down to me, he gave me a good solid 'high-five.' "Nice to meet you, little girl," he said. He was very hospitable; Betty quickly made the introductions, and in a soft heartfelt voice Sasha said,

"Well, it's so nice to have the both of you here, let me give you guys a quick tour of my pad." He took us in and showed us all around, the ground floor was a trendy rustic cafe, just for coffees and snacks y'know, the first floor was a charming little restaurant, mainly used by tourists in the spring and summer months, (it had a modern deluxe kitchen built in the back). The second floor was Sasha's private living space, a nice snazzy apartment filled with classy Italian furniture, and above that was a cosy little roof terrace, Sasha had it all kitted-out nicely, with a stone pizza barbecue, a pink bubbling Jacuzzi, an old wooden picnic bench, and a little greenhouse with solar panels. He grew all his own herbs and spices up there, this wizard really knew how to look after himself. When we got back down to the ground floor, I suddenly felt quite hot, so I decided to take my red jacket off, and that's when Sasha saw the fresh blood on my ripped-up T-shirt.

"Ahhhh, so you're the one who's given my rib a new home eh, I actually felt the rib call to me, when you guys first touched it, you woke it up from a deep sleep, y'know." Sasha's deep

'Barry-White' voice sounded bold and powerful, and his eyes were different colours, one was light blue and the other dark green, I noticed how they changed shades in the sunlight. This guy looked nothing like a wizard, he certainly didn't dress or act like one; he wore old Levi's 501 jeans and a navy T-shirt. He dropped down to one knee again, and looking quite humble he said, "Louise, I just want to say that... I'm deeply sorry for dragging you into all this craziness, and I'm sorry about your rib being removed. That must have been an awful experience for you?" He turned to Betty now.

"My darling daughter, Betty. I need to apologies to you too honey. Please forgive me for being such a secretive old recluse for all these years. I just couldn't let anyone know I was living out here; it would have been too dangerous for all of us, I hope you understand." Sasha suddenly became teary-eyed and emotional again, he decided to cough a few times, to try and cover up his feelings, then he smiled a magnificent gleam that seemed to make him look like an old Hollywood actor called Gene Kelly. I used to love watching Gene Kelly dance with Jerry the Mouse in 'Anchors Aweigh.' The old films are the best, that's what my Mum always says. Sasha's eager eyes, along with his fidgety body language, suggested that he now had something new to say. He gently wrapped his big strong arms around the both of us and said.

"I would be very honoured if you two lovely ladies joined me for a spot of lunch in the mountains," he sighed.

It was impossible for Sasha to hide his love for Betty.

Every time he looked at her, his face sparkled with delight.

"Lunch sounds lovely." I said.

"Yes, I agree," said Betty, in her kind un-bossy lady-like voice.

An important question suddenly popped-up in my head. "Hey Sasha, what about Roaring Meg?"

"Isn't she up on the moon right now trying to free all those nasty witches?" Sasha started to laugh out loud.

"She most certainly is, Louise, but I wouldn't worry too much about her, it's going to be extremely hard and difficult for her to open those marble prison gates."

Sasha giggled wildly, like an excited kid.

"I made an adjustment spell, you see." Betty and I looked at each other with curious eyes. "What's an adjustment spell?" I asked. "It's really easy to understand," he said.

"I've called this particular spell the 'INTERNET FRUSTRATION SPELL,' let me explain, please sit." Sasha gestured us towards the round little coffee table that sat all alone by the cafe's main entrance, it was half covered by yellow strands of flimsy jasmine branches, once seated Sasha spontaneously got up and ran back indoors to fetch a single sunflower in a tiny vase, and after placing it on the table, he quickly zoomed back off again, only to return with three small glasses filled with sweet lemon iced-tea.

We sipped on our cool drinks and patiently waited for this whimsical wizard to explain things in more detail.

"Ok ladies, the magnificent internet frustration spell goes like this, let me explain, so, the only time I need to go online these days is when I'm ordering stuff for my cafe, usually coffee and sugar, anyway, the internet is terribly slow up here in the mountains, and this drives me nuts, it's a real bummer y'know. I know wizards should be patient and mellow-minded, but I have no time for stuff like that." Sasha suddenly started to perform a silly little dance, then he laughed out loud, this guy was overflowing with love and happiness, I swear. He went on, "Ok, so, there I was, ordering stuff online about a year ago, and I had just quit smoking the week before, so I needed to be doing something with my hands y'know, I needed to keep my mind off the smokey-smokes. So, I decided to throw an old baseball up against the wall, just to catch it again and again. So there I was, online, waiting for my 'stock-up' order to say, ORDER COMPLETE. The hours dragged by, and all my patience ran out, after two hundred minutes of waiting, I got so angry and frustrated, that I started squeezing my baseball like King Kong, I used it like a stress ball, and by sheer accident I filled it up with raw magic. I squeezed that baby with all my thunder, and to my astonishment, it grew. After twenty minutes of mad monk squeezing, it grew bigger than a frickin basketball."

Sasha simmered down for a sec, and we all sipped on our iced-tea at the exact same time, this made us laugh a bit, he went on. "That huge ball got completely filled-up with anger, magic and frustration, and it grew so big that I ended up crushing it into fine dust, I tipped all the dust into an old shoe bag and gave it to Max, and soon after that he took it up to the moon and proceeded to sprinkle this fine INTERNET FRUSTRATION DUST all over the main gates of the marble prison." Sasha was giggling again, laughing uncontrollably like a drunk hyena, he fell off his chair, and quickly got back up to explain things. "I put two spells on that unique dust, the first spell was to keep the prison gates closed for as long as possible, and the second spell was to curse whoever came along, by infecting them with all the anger and frustration inside the dust." Sasha was in hysterics, he laughed like an 'old-school' cartoon character called…'Muttley' a dog from the wacky races. "Poor old Meg, she's gonna be so stressed-out up there on the moon. It's gonna take her a long time to free those witches, I know that much, the dust will curse her bones with anger and irritation. She's gonna feel riddled beyond reason, ha!" Sasha was very pleased with himself, he couldn't stop himself from dancing about, he stood up and did the moonwalk like Michael Jackson, he was funny to watch. Then, quite unexpectedly, a young Italian kid flew past the cafe on a powerful Kawasaki motorbike. Sweet Mary

Poppins! He just missed Sasha by two inches, phew-wee. Betty rolled her eyes-up, her father's emotions and zany behaviour was all over the place, she asked,
"How long will this INTERNET FRUSTRATION SPELL last, Daddy-O?" Sasha replied,
"It will push all Meg's plans back for three days. Don't worry, my love. We have more than enough time." It was my turn to ask a question now. "Hey Sasha, you said MAX took all the fine dust up to the moon. Well, I'm curious, who is Max?" Sasha quickly put his finger and thumb up to his lips, he whistled out a quick loud tune, and two seconds later the red robin wearing the bomber hat flew over and landed on his shoulder. "This is my best friend, Max Redwood, he's a super confident little red-chested robin, born in London. I found Max about twelve years ago, he was dead on the road, about two miles away from the cafe, he got squashed into the tarmac by a ten ton French lorry. I felt sorry for the flat little dude, so I decided to use some purple magic on him, just enough to bring him back to life, y'know." Sasha closed his eyes tightly, there was a child-like innocence oozing out from his heart, he was thinking deeply, I guess he was digging out an old memory, right from the back of his mind. "Ah yes, I remember exactly what happened now, I only wanted to give Max a little dose of purple magic, just enough to make his tiny heart start beating again, but something happened.

It's easy to bring a little robin back to life, you only need the tiniest pinch of purple magic, well, this was the intended desire, but something caught me off guard just before I cast the spell, I caught a whiff of some wild mountain lavender, and accidentally released a huge supersonic-power-blasting-hurricane-sneeze. This sneeze ended up blessing Max with an obscene amount of purple magic, it lingered all around him for ages, making him glow up like a purple Jedi lightsaber. The little robin dude received over a hundred times more purple magic than he actually needed, and this resulted in him turning out to be an ultra cool, highly advanced supersonic interesting robin with untold powers. That sneeze was the best mistake I ever made. Ha-ha!" Max whistled in agreement. Sasha giggled, then he rambled on like a salesman.

"Max can fly faster than a speeding bullet, he can breathe underwater, speak ten different languages, carry logs, make crisps, serve customers, make cappuccinos, keep the greenhouse clean and bug-free. He's very talented in the kitchen, he makes a mean minestrone soup, a boombastic banana beef lasagna, and his thin crust pepperoni pizzas are out of this world, flippin phenomenal. Speaking of food, I think it's high-time we had some lunch." Sasha suddenly started to sing a silly little song. I think he was making it all up as he went along. *"Oh, lunch-time with my Betty, do you fancy some spaghetti? Cos that's what you're gonna-getti. Wiggly spaghetti for Louise and Betty, a squeeze of lemon if you're hot and sweaty. And the parmesan cheese will bring you to your knees, if you please, Louise. Ha ha!"* Silly Sasha was so happy to be re-united with his daughter. Betty had a big sunny smile all over her face too. It was an absolute pleasure hanging out with these cool cosmic cats. I had to pinch myself - one minute I was off to the laundromat, to wash my grubby school clothes on a cold wet night, and now I was in Italy, having lunch with a cool wizard, along side his beautiful eccentric daughter, and I was also in the presence of a living legend, Max Redwood the magnificent robin; I was having a great time, and the sun was shining too. What a sweet bonus. I wish England had more sunshine, oh well. Sasha suddenly dashed back inside again, he flew up the stairs and kept himself very busy, preparing a fantastic lunch for us. I saw him cooking through the window, he was dancing and jolting around like Mick Jagger; the old dude couldn't keep still, my first Italian lunch was on it's way, yeh-baby! It was cool and windy out, typical March weather I guess, we decided to brave the breeze and stay outside, it was the naked blue skies that won us over, they helped take the edge off the chilly temperatures, having the sun on our backs kind of tricked us into thinking it was May or June, toasty sunlight vitamin D charging us up, it was very soothing, the strong winds got pretty wild though. We had vegetable soup for starters, served with fresh crusty olive ciabatta bread. Deee-lish! "Get it while it's hot," shouted Sasha. It truly was utterly scrumptious. Then came the main course: magnificent meatballs served with fresh wiggly spaghetti bolognese, the whole plate was covered by a blizzard of parmesan cheese. This beautiful fresh Italian food really hit the spot; it was super yummy. I must say, I got a little bit freaked out when I saw how the spaghetti danced on my plate."Hey what's that all about? Why is my food moving?" "Ah, that's just a tiny pinch of purple magic mixed with fresh lime juice. It makes the pasta wiggle like worms, it gives the dish a nice zesty-ping-ting-whizz-kick taste." It made my eyes squint and water big time, but it was very tasty. Eating this special spaghetti made me feel like I had dancing disco worms going down the hatch; it was a tickly affair. After we ate, Sasha wanted to enlighten us about some of his strange cooking habits.

"I have two types of meatballs," he said.

"First, we have the delicious kind that we've all just enjoyed for lunch." Sasha quickly snapped his fingers, and Max flew off to the kitchen.

"The other type I have are these new rare ones - they're exploding meatballs." Max flew back out with a huge salad bowl perfectly balanced on his little robin head; the big bowl was filled with extra-large exploding meatballs.

"These exploding little beauties will be perfect ammunition for when we fight against the crazy witch army, they're going to come in very handy, no doubt about it. They explode into potent sleeping smoke, the strong effective substance inside will knock any witch out cold, for two days. We can definitely use these meatballs when the time comes. I also have some exploding sausages, real big banger bombs, they work just the same way." Sasha's voice suddenly became more serious. "A battle is coming my dear compadres, the witches are going to be knocking on our door very soon, believe me, I'm speaking the truth here, I tell ya no lies, Roaring Meg, along with her witch army, are determined to rule the whole world, they want to keep people living in doubt and fear every day."

Sasha gave us both the eyeball for a moment, just to emphasise his point, he was dishing out the cold facts all right. He went on, "They're going to want to fight and kill all of us, but have no fears my dears, old Pops has a wham-bam-killer-plan. We're going to call on THE FUZZ CATS and THE PARADOX TWINS for back-up. No doubt these guys will help us take care of all the business we need to cover, they'll come out of the shadows for sure."

I had no idea what Sasha was talking about now.

"What's a Fuzz Cat?" I asked.

Sasha gently walked behind my chair and proceeded to give me a three-second shoulder rub. It was nice, but way too short. He rambled on some more.

"I will tell you all about these magnificent fuzzy weirdos soon my dear, but right now it's time for dessert, followed by coffee and biscuits."

Max suddenly flew off into the kitchen again, only to return with a huge silver dessert tray balanced on his head, he carried a perfect-looking homemade tiramisu, but the little guy dropped it on Betty's head, oops-a-daisy. Betty looked like she'd just lost a passionate food fight in a cake factory. We helped clean her up in no time; she saw the funny side of it, thank goodness, the tiramisu held Betty's hair in position stronger than any hair wax ever could, only some of it went to waste. I'm pleased to report that Max was more successful when he delivered the coffees and biscuits, silly robin. Over a flat white coffee, Sasha explained how he had a fantastic plan, he called it his Masterplan. I will tell you more about that soon. Sasha had so much to say. "First off, we need Betty and Max to go fetch The Fuzz Cats and The Paradox Twins. This will probably take twenty-four hours, these guys are not just around the corner. The Fuzz Cats live in East London and The Paradox Twins live in two separate locations: one lives in a forest, in Alaska, and the other lives at the bottom of the Atlantic Ocean." Sasha had great confidence in his masterplan. "Louise, I want you to stay here with me please. The last seventeen hours of your life have been quite wild and wacky, to say the least. You've definitely earned yourself some down-time. You can help out in the kitchen if you like. I'm gonna make a big feast for when the wrecking crew returns." Sasha started to clear the table, he was about to disappear back inside the coffee shop, when he suddenly stopped dead in his tracks, turning back to us, he now looked ready to share some great bold words of wisdom and encouragement.

"Ladies, the time has come for us to create a tenacious gang," he spritefully agreed with himself.

"YES… A BOOMBASTIC-HARDCORE TENACIOUS GANG. A TRUE BLUE SCOOBY DOO WRECKING CREW." Sasha smiled like his face had just been picked to go on the front cover of Rolling Stone magazine.

He raised his fist up high and quickly punched the air like a rugged passionate rock star. He said one more thing, "TENACIOUS TEAM-WORK MAKES THE AUDACIOUS DREAM-WORK! YEH-BABY, YOU KNOW IT'S TRUE, COME ON MY SON!" Then he disappeared off into the coffee shop, but he was back after two minutes, with a small piece of paper in his hand.

"Here you go, Betty. I have here the full address of The Fuzz Cats residence, over in East London."

Betty knocked her coffee back, hopped-up on her jet-powered-rocket-ironing-board, typed the address into her mini sat nav-system, looked at me and her Papa, and said, "See ya later alligator," and half a second later she flew off into the distance, just like a golf ball being whacked down the fairway. Max Redwood took flight as well, he zoomed-off right behind her. I think he overtook her, it was hard to tell cos both these speed-racers were out of sight in seconds. Betty headed straight for London, while Max flew further out to Alaska. Standing straight and strong, Sasha watched-on as he admired his daughter's dynamite speed.

"My O My, look at her go. Ahhhh … That's my girl."

This wondrous wizard was happy again, his positive emotions of bold joy were rubbing off on me, and it felt great, this was just what I needed, some happy vibes to help keep my heart rich, excellent. Thank you kindly, Mr Sonic, awfully nice of ya, ha-ha. Right, what's next?

CHAPTER 10
CHARGE THOSE BATTERIES UP

I made myself a hot chocolate in the coffee bar while Sasha went upstairs to the kitchen, he suggested I go up to the roof terrace and just chill for a while, he knew I needed some time to rest, plus, he wanted to get started on the big feast. I enjoyed a lazy afternoon up on that luxurious roof, it was a groovy feeling, Sasha played Louis Armstrong and Ella Fitzgerald all through the afternoon. Kicking back under the sun was just what I needed, I'd experienced way too much stress and trauma. I ventured over to the greenhouse, walked in, and had a good look around, it was full of life in there, the mint leaves smelt wonderful, and the big bold sunflowers looked gorgeous, Sasha grew them all year round. The muggy sultry air inside kind of left me feeling drowsy, I had to get out, it was too hot and moist. Back outside I gawped at the pink Jacuzzi tub, it looked so inviting, there was a subtle chill on the breeze now, it kind of disturbed my inner peace, made me want to jump in.

"Oh yeh baby. I've got to have a dip in that hot mama," I whispered to myself. I quickly yelled downstairs, asking Sasha if it was okey to have a little paddle in the pink tub.

"Of course you can, that's what it's there for," he shouted.

"Knock yourself out, Louise." He wasn't kidding.

Half a minute later, Sasha threw a big navy 'Nike' sports bag up onto the roof terrace, it just missed my head. D'oh. "Here you go," he shouted. "Thanks, Sasha." I replied. Inside I found a variety of soft jumbo towels, and a cool red ladybird dressing gown, it had huge black dots all over it. Sasha stayed in the kitchen for hours, he was cooking up a storm of snacks and tapas. I couldn't see him, but I heard his voice singing with Louis and Ella; it poured upwards spilling out the window like steam, keeping me company all through the afternoon, it was a delightful joyous background noise, the cheery vocal vibes changed the air around me. Sasha reminded me so much of Betty. Sweet heavens above, that hot Jacuzzi was ace; in fact, it was a bit too relaxing. When I couldn't take any more, I stepped out and quickly slipped into the red dotty dressing gown, then I walked down into Sasha's apartment, leaving wet footprints on the shiny wooden floor behind me, I got nice and comfortable on his posh Italian sofa, then I put a DVD on, I watched an old 1956 movie called 'Bus Stop,' it was great, then I slipped into a snooze. That dip in the tub really knocked me out, sweet Moses, I slept for fourteen hours. I had no idea I was so tired. I guess my body still wanted to recover from the 'rib-transplant' operation, it took its toll on me y'know. I guess I was still a bit shook-up, the purple magic helped. I woke up all sprawled out on that comfy sofa, It was a blissful feeling, I was happy to find myself under a big soft ' blue and white' stripy duvet, I guess Sasha threw it over me while I slept like a baby, how thoughtful. I felt dopey and dreamy, but after taking a few deep breaths, I got up and shuffled downstairs to wish Sasha a good morning. Walking through the restaurant area, I noticed a lovely burning fireplace in the corner. It crackled and whispered lots of cosy popping sounds; it made the whole room feel warm and homely. I soon found Sasha making breakfast in his posh kitchen. There was a great song blasting out the radio, 'A Beautiful Morning' by The Rascals. "Good morning, Louise. Did you sleep well? The rest of the gang will definitely be coming back today, just before sundown I reckon." Sasha was cheerful and chirpy as ever. "Good morning, Sasha. That sounds great, I look forward to meeting everyone later, and yes, I slept very well thank you. Oh, and thanks for the duvet, that was very kind of you." I still felt mushy and spongy in my head. I needed ten more minutes to wake up properly. Sasha smiled, then he asked me a question that nobody had ever asked me before in my entire life.

"Would you like some octopus tentacles on toast?"

"Wow, I've never had a breakfast like that before. Yes, I think I'll give it a try." This kind of breakfast had a real twing-twang-twist to it, get ready taste buds. Sasha looked at me with vivid eyes and said,

"Would you like to add some wasabi, just to spice things up a little?"

"Oh, no thanks," I said. I wasn't too sure about all this, but then I paused. "Oh, go on then, maybe just a cheeky pinch.""Yes, that's the spirit," said the bohemian wizard. "It's good to push yourself and try new things from time to time, Louise." He winked at me. I agreed with Sasha, but this time the wasabi was too much. I had to quickly gulp down a cold glass of water. Sasha made me a nice bowl of frosted flakes after that, I waited till the flakes were just right, not too crispy, not too soggy, they had to sit in the milk for just the right amount of time, Italian milk taste different from English milk. I love placing my hands over my ears when I chew on my corn flakes, you should try it. Sasha's colourful kitchen was full of pictures and hanging pots and pans, it had so much character. I looked around and quickly noticed several polaroid shots of Max Redwood, they were blu-tacked on the big fridge door. He had a red SMEG fridge. It looked pretty cool.

"Hey Sasha, can you tell me more about Max Redwood?"

"Yes, of course, I'd be happy to, Max first moved from London to Suffolk when he was two, he's the type of robin who gets bored of things quickly y'know. I guess that's why he flew out to Italy, to find some new adventures. He fell in love with 'Italia' in seconds; he loves green olives, Italian breadsticks, and all the birds, and he sleeps in the greenhouse." Sasha reached into the fridge for some fresh tropicana tropical fruit juice, he pour me a glass, it was nice and cold. "Hey, Louise, can you help me with this pasta sauce please? Just keep stirring it for the next ten minutes." I was happy to help Sasha, it was fun being in the kitchen with a wizard; he had many dishes on the go. Sasha kept busy rambling on about Max while he crushed several garlic cloves and chopped-up lots of mozzarella cheese blobs. "Max is very happy here in Italy y'know, he's always reading books while sunbathing up on the roof, the sun has turned his orange chest to a dark red wine scarlet colour." Sasha now turned his attention to making a huge supersize thin-crust-vegetarian-pizza, he was shaping the fresh dough with great skill, spinning and throwing it up high, catching it like it was nothing. He went on…"Max once told me how he still loves going back to England, just once a year, to visit his folks in October. He loves getting a good lungful of the cold English countryside air. He's got a very interesting home back in Suffolk; his folks still live there today. It's an old rusty broken-down tractor, sitting on the edge of a field, half-hidden in the bushes. It looks totally abandoned on the outside; but on the inside it's a secret hideout custom-made luxurious apartment, built specifically for robins. Piece by piece, Max removed the whole engine, he slowly filled the empty space with lego, hay, hacky-sack balls and fairy lights. Hacky sack balls make great bean bags for robins y'know. Max kept himself busy ripping all the sponge out from the old

tractor's driving seat, and after a lot of pecking, he turned random bits of chunky sponge into tiny miniature beds and armchairs, how cool is that? It's really snug and cosy in there." Sasha pointed to one of the polaroids on the cherry red fridge door. "Here, look." It was a picture of Max standing proudly on top of his tractor-home. Sasha gave Max the thumbs up.
"That old run-down tractor is a damn good find y'know. Max has always been a resourceful little fellow, he once found an old electric blanket dumped in a skip, and with a little bit of help from his cousins, he took it home, trimmed it down and connected it up to the car battery that was still attached to the old tractor, and like magic, the electric blanket heated the secret apartment right up, it's been great for those long cold winter nights. That blanket has kept their secret home warm for many winters now, he's a brainy one, old Max."

"But how does Max keep the car battery charged-up?" I asked this with sincere concern. Sasha smiled and said,
"Well, I went over there once, to help set up a unique antenna that attracts lightning, so every time they have a thunderstorm in Suffolk, the battery gets fully charged up, I did this for his folks, it seems to work, so far so good. Max doesn't have any siblings by the way, he's an only robin, but he does have lots of cool cousins, and they love coming to Italy for their summer holidays. They visit every year, usually around the middle of

July. The greenhouse up on the roof terrace gets over-crowded every time they come, so, using random bits of smashed-up wood found from an old deserted beach hut, Max build them a nice little hotel. 'The Max Redwood Hotel,' it sits on an old railway sleeper just outside, Max built it a couple of years ago." Sasha pointed at another polaroid on the fridge door. It was Max and his cousin, Antonio (the one flappin in the background). This photo was taken last summer.

(Dear Reader, please go to youtube and play the "Max Redwood" song).

It was crystal clear to see that Sasha loves his little robin buddy. They've been best mates for years. For the average man, they say his best friend is his dog. But for a cool wizard like Sasha, his best friend was definitely Max Redwood the Magnificent Robin. Sasha always says....

"You just can't keep a good robin down," He shared a silly bird joke with me, "Hey Louise, where does Woody Woodpecker live? Peckham!" Oh no, that's a terrible joke.

CHAPTER 11

THE PARADOX TWINS

For over an hour I stirred that frick'in pasta sauce, while Sonic Sasha happily blabbered away about all kinds of things. He suddenly paused and said…"Louise Buttersky, it's time for you and I to enjoy some delicious ice cream." He reached into the freezer and pulled out a tub of home-made-high-quality-mint-choc-chip-Italiano-gelato, using his special ice cream scoopy scoop spoon, he filled two bowls up, topping them off with crushed cashew nuts mixed with hot chocolate sauce. Holy smoking pancakes, it was molto buona - magnifico! Now I knew for sure, that I had come to the right place, no doubt in my mind. Still in my ladybird dressing gown, I perched myself up on a kitchen stool and got busy scoffing, a short way into my dessert I stopped and asked Sasha to fill me in on 'The Paradox Twins,' I was curious to know about these guys. Who were they, and what were they all about?

"Sure, of course I'd be happy to tell you all about the Paradox Twins," said Sasha with ice cream all over his lips. "We need to go way back in time to fully understand how these two strange dudes actually came into existence." Sasha coughed to clear his throat.

"Ok, Louise, listen carefully please. It goes like this… It was early March in 1964 when Roaring Meg carried out some rather radical experiments, in her North Londonwitch cave, that dark morbid tatty old warehouse. I believe you've been there, haven't you?" Sasha winked at me, I rolled my eyes up, then he went on, "Meg's plan was simple, she wanted to make a special key that would allow her to successfully unlock the marble prison gates, the old girl created a new key every night, she flew up to the moon with her fingers crossed, and gave it her best shot to open those massive gates, but nothing ever happened, because ALL the keys she made were a complete load of metal mumbo jumbo!" Sasha laughed out loud. "Feeling angry, defeated, and completely frustrated, Meg would fly back to her witch-cave and go completely berserk with pure witch-rage, she'd smash and obliterate pretty much everything she owned, she destroyed a brand new TV every week. This became a regular routine for Meg; the rats living in that warehouse thought she was losing her marbles. She'd get so angry that her eyes would turn a deep fiery red crimson colour, and one day, they just stayed that way." Sasha knew he had my full attention, I couldn't stop gazing at him with my mouth wide open, I took in every word he said, I had a huge blob of Italian ice cream spilled down my ladybird dressing gown, but I knew nothing about it, I only found out when Sasha gently scooped it off and ate it, he continued with the story, explaining things nice and slow. Please proceed Mr Sonic,

"After repeating this pattern nearly a hundred times,

old Meg came to an intense breaking-point, she smashed big holes in the walls of her warehouse, and shorty after that, the nutty old bat turned to the booze, she became a hardcore-whiskey-loving-zit-face-alcoholic, and of course this only made matters worse - it was like she turned into the Queen of Rage overnight. It got to the point where she became so sick of making rubbish keys, that she decided to try something completely different, and that was the day she attempted to make TWO SUPERSONIC BODYGUARDS, this turned out to be a highly disastrous experiment, she screwed everything up right from the get-go. Both bodyguards ended up becoming THE PARADOX TWINS. I will explain how it all happened." I was enjoying Sasha's storytelling, all that was missing was a camp fire and some stars shining above. Mr Sonic continued, "Using two large test tubes, Meg got busy mixing a wide variety of unorthodox ingredients: she used things like crocodile blood, crushed tiger teeth, wolf claws soaked in snake-blood mixed with apple cider vinegar, shredded seaweed from the Bermuda Triangle, vampire bones soaked in pirate rum, taste buds from a dead lion's tongue, old bogies from a dead grizzly bear's nose, piranha-fish teeth, some hair from Albert Einstein's moustache, wasp blood, stingray skin, and some chopped up electric eels." Sasha was still enjoying his ice cream. I needed a break from mine; I had a full-on-mouth-freeze. He went on.

"Now, on the morning of the big, 'BODYGUARD EXPERIMENT,' Meg stupidly drank three bottles of whiskey, and after lunch she downed a bottle of vodka.

Her drinking had gotten way out of control." Sasha suddenly looked straight into my eyes, "Remember this Louise, it's never a good idea to perform dangerous intense science experiments when you're completely sloshed on whiskey, especially when magic and witch spells are involved." Sasha tapped his silver ice cream spoon firmly against mine. CLINK! "Science, magic and whiskey don't mix together well at all. That's a fact, Jack!" Sasha quickly snapped his fingers and pointed both his dandy hands at me, posing like a dotty old dancing disco diva. "Meg's whole approach to this experiment was pathetic, completely unprofessional – a perfect example of tragic-magic. Instead of making two supersonic bodyguards, she accidentally ended up creating two highly unorthodox creatures, and these guys turned out to be… The Paradox Twins. Now, lots of kids and adults believe that 'The Paradox Twins' are just two spooky characters from old scary bedtime stories, but the truth is, THEY ARE REAL! They really do exist, Louise." Sasha smiled like a swotty little 'know-it-all' genius.

"The first Twin goes by the name of Leon. He's a fierce blood-thirsty-wolf-man – a wild virile creature, half werewolf - half vampire, a gruesome hairy beast with bigfangs and hot sizzling lava lion blood running through his veins. He can walk through fire and go a whole year without food. His eyes are icy blue and his face looks like rough tree bark, he's ridiculously strong." Oh I say, Leon sounds scary, I had chills tingling all over me. "Over the years, many men have tried to kill Leon, but no-one has ever succeeded. He's been shot many times, but he'll never die because he's completely un-killable, he's an old rugged hobo, his heart is pure liquid silver. Now, there's an old saying that says... werewolves can only be killed by a silver bullet, well, this rule doesn't apply to Leon. Every time he gets shot by a silver bullet, it just melts down into liquid, and quickly travels straight to his heart, silver bullets actually make this cat stronger, crazy hey. The vampire side of Leon is also pretty insane, he loves blood; he eats Alaskan cougars and grizzly bears quite often. Leon escaped from Meg's witch cave when he was two months old. He decided to live in Alaska because it's nice and peaceful up there, I have no idea how he got there, he's been living alone in the snow for the last fifty years, in an old deserted church, in the middle of a gigantic sequoia forest. Nobody ever disturbs him, he lives off the grid, little Max will find him, that robin has a very unique gift when it comes to communicating with tough warriors, he seems to have some kind of 'Tinkerbell-Aura' that wins them over every time, he knows how to cut straight to the heart, you can feel it when he sings." I sighed for a moment. "Wow, Leon sounds cool, Sasha." I was well impressed, then, quite suddenly, Sasha started to panic. "Hey, wait a minute, there he is now! Just over there. Look, that's Leon outside, running towards us! Oh dear, he looks terribly angry!"

"What? Where? Where is he!?" I pushed Sasha out of the way and quickly jumped-up to have a look-see out the kitchen window, I badly wanted to see this Vampire-Wolf-Man. My speedy heart-beat suddenly doubled it's pace.

I looked out the window, but saw no one, and by the time I parked my bum back on my stool, I realised that Sasha had successfully stolen the remainder of my mint-choc-chip-gelato-ice cream, cheeky sod, how rude! I was really enjoying the cold minty puddle at the bottom of my bowl, oh well. "Ha-ha. Gotcha!" Cried Sasha.

"Yeah-yeah, nice one, Sasha, you got me there." What a Poo-head. This wacky wizard had the playful spirit of a dolphin. I suddenly started thinking long and hard about Leon.

"I kind of feel sorry for Leon," I said.

"He must get awfully lonely up in that Alaskan forest." I felt nervous about meeting him, he sounded like a weirdo. Sasha's raw description led me to believe that he was a killer. The Beast from the East: that's what they call him in the United States. I couldn't believe that this hairy freak was coming to join us for dinner, I hope he doesn't eat me. Wouldn't that be an unpleasant way to go. "I hope Leon has better table manners than you, Sasha," I jokingly said. The old wizard soon picked-up on my nervous feelings, he didn't miss a thing, he remained cool and calm, as usual.

"Ahhhh, don't worry about Leon, he's alright. I know how to handle him. He just needs a bit of tough love, that's all, he needs a father figure. I'll keep a good eye on him, don't you worry, Lou-Bee-Lou. Some freshly cooked Italian food will straighten him out in no time." I certainly hope so. I had a new job in the kitchen now, Sasha put me in charge of all the salad, but first I ran upstairs to put my jeans back on, I felt silly looking like a big ladybird all morning, I decided to borrow one of Sasha's t-shirts. When I came back down Mr Sonic handed me a small knife, he told me to chop the cucumbers, cut all the baby tomatoes in half, and slice and dice the big iceberg lettuce. "Be careful with that knife, Louise – it's a sharp little cutter." I took caution, and started chopping. Sasha was now making some kind of weird fresh banana beef lasagna, a 'Max Redwood speciality.' Stopping to make coffee, he turned the volume of the radio up, it was a throwback sixties-show, after that he topped-up my glass of tropicana fruit juice, Sasha now looked ready to tell me about the other Paradox Twin. "Ok, Louise, it's time for me to give you a rundown on 'Tigerlips.' A strange ferocious sea-cat, one-third tiger, one-third electric eel, and one-third stingray, and just like his brother, he turned out to be a pretty damn cool creation, these two peculiar super-freaks are the only good things that ever came from Meg's constant boozing, but being the heartless tart she is, Meg abandoned Tiger when he was only three weeks old, she dropped him in the River Thames when he was no bigger than a kitten, the wild undercurrents soon dragged him out to the estuary of the open sea, but that wasn't a problem for this wild-cat, he survived, his spirit is crazy strong, he just kept swimming and swimming, and in a short stretch of time he developed some pretty effective hunting skills, I tell ya, this cat never went hungry, he caught all kinds of fish. The big bold ocean quickly became Tiger's home, he's been living out at sea his whole life." Sasha sipped on his coffee, then he rambled on some more. "Tiger lives on the flat seabed way out in the deepest coldest parts of the Atlantic Ocean, he created a home inside the rusty remains of the old Titanic shipwreck. He loves that song... 'I will Survive' by Gloria Gaynor" Sasha's head suddenly bowed down, like he was attending a funeral or something. He felt sad for Tiger, cos he was always alone. He sounded pretty awesome to me. A tiger with gills, that's crazy!

"Staying inside that old shipwreck almost all the time is no way to live, Louise. It's dark, cold and haunted down there, I swear. Who wants to be living all alone down at the bottom of the freezing cold ocean? It's unhealthy. A Tiger needs stimulating company from time to time, that shabby old shipwreck is nothing but a ghostly old tomb."

Sasha suddenly moved in closer, looking like he was about to spill the beans on some top-secret-information.

"Louise, I must tell you something... I've been secretly stashing lots of purple magic down in that shipwreck for many years, the purple magic keeps Tiger sharp and strong, this is my way of helping him." I understood exactly what Sasha meant, cos I now had purple magic in my system, and it felt great! This guy's rib saved my life. It was like having a calm relaxing flow of gentle electricity swimming in my bloodstream, all the time, pure heaven."

Sasha explained things in more detail.

"Max Redwood has secretly been delivering small doses of purple magic to that old shipwreck for years now. I knew that, one day, I was going to need that cool sea-cat for something. Well, come dinner time tonight, Tiger will be a unique member of our brand new tenacious gang. All the purple magic around the Titanic has gotten under his skin, it has also seeped-deep into the ships rusty body, this is the main reason why Tiger still likes living down there today. The energy-force down there is beautiful, and plentiful."

"That old shipwreck now has a positive highly-charged-buzz, all over it, it's completely surrounded by unique abundant vibrations, oozing out a mellow ambience." Sasha was very pleased with himself. He stood like a proud superhero, who was about to receive an 'Oscar' for shrewd thinking, he gently tapped his nose before giving me a nudge and a wink. I understood exactly what he meant - mom's the word, be hush hush about all this, don't tell a soul. Who would I tell anyway? And even if I did tell someone, what would they do? They'd probably think I was nuts! Sasha sang along to the songs on the radio now, while chopping through some red peppers, he was perky and jumpy, he couldn't keep still to save his life; I think that was the coffee, he always had an espresso on the go, just like bonsai-Betty. Sasha suddenly stopped chopping the peppers and reached over to adjust the oven, this was a very trippy moment for me, I will explain, the knife he let go of continued chopping the peppers all by itself. Wizard magic is soooo cooooooooool! I had something I wanted to say to Sasha now,

"The Paradox Twins sound like a couple of dark dudes Sasha, but they also sound very unique and interesting."

"Yes, they are very dark dudes indeed, they have some serious issues, the trouble is this, they both feel completely ripped-off and abandoned by Meg you see, they're still extremely angry with her. That rotten drunk loser is the closest thing they've got to a mother, how sad is that?" Sasha had a point, this was a very sad fact to ponder over. He rambled on some more. "Given half the chance, they'd probably rip her head off and roast her corpse over a campfire, out in the woods." Sasha was smiling when he said this, but there was an element of truth in his words, they'd probably overcook her and feed her to the bears. Sasha made light of things when he said,

"Ah, they'll be alright, they just need a 'Pack' to belong to – and we can help with that." Sasha went on to explain how The Paradox Twins turn stronger when they hang out together. They are highly advanced powerful individuals, but when they're together, a connection of high potent synergy comes into play, they're like a lethal force of nature, with very high IQs. I was very pleased to know that these dangerous brothers were going to be on our side, and not with the mini witches. Sasha sipped on his large espresso some more, he spoke up again.

"As I said earlier… Tiger and Leon were created back in early March, 1964, and they ALWAYS get together on their birthday, so with a bit of luck, they'll both be in Alaska; this will make things easier for Max. He'll find both these dudes in Leon's church, in the sequoia forest. They'll be playing cards and smoking big cigars, that's their usual birthday tradition, it's become a bit of a ritual. They have a typical love-hate brother relationship, kind of like the, "Oasis brothers." Sasha rolled his eyes up,

"I know The Paradox Twins will be happy to join forces with us. I don't think they want to be a pair of 'roaming outcasts' anymore, they need a unique purpose to fulfil."
Sasha suddenly squeezed my shoulder.
"They'll be happy to join forces with us," he smiled, and a moment later he was looking out the kitchen window, for a very long time. He gazed and gazed for a good two minutes, like an Irish poet absorbing inspiration, he suddenly delivered a little speech. "We are destined to become a wild tenacious gang, crazy and strong enough to stand up to Roaring Meg, and all those twisted mini witches." Sasha quickly made a little poem on the spot.
"The only thing, that's never been seen, is the true SPIRIT of an unbreakable team." It sounded like a prayer, or a sermon. Sasha took the deepest breath, he slowly sighed.
"Yes, that's us, Louise. That's us," I patted Sasha on the back. "You da man, Sonic-Sasha!" I was trying to be extra confident. Sasha smiled down at me, then he looked up to the ceiling, I think he was digging out an old memory.

"Ah yes, I remember now. Three years ago, I gave a nice Christmas present to Leon – a flying Triumph motorbike called 'IRON JOHN.' It's a loud gutsy runner with an aerodynamic sidecar, a one of a kind retro dynamite roadster. Betty built it for me back in 69, but I never really used it all that much, so I gave it to Leon.

'IRON JOHN' will get them here safely."

Leon's flying motorbike

Taking a break from all the wacky chit-chat, Sasha re-directed his attention to the amazing dishes he was preparing. The kitchen was filled with many rich authentic Italian aromas, home-made wizardry cooking at it's best. I suddenly got hit by a feeling inside, it was like I had a sort of awakening, a new awareness of a new connection. I suddenly realised that I felt everything Sasha felt, this connection was kind of like the bond Elliot had with ET, in that old movie. This was a new gift from my special rib, the rib *was* a part of Sasha after all. The bond we had was growing fast, we got on famously well.

Deep inside, I felt that Sasha genuinely wanted to help Leon and Tigerlips; he's a damn good man y'know, a cool wizard, and a street-wise gentleman, all rolled into one, God bless his big bold heart. Sasha knew too well that these unorthodox twins were just a couple of heart-broken black-sheep weirdos, destined to become born-again heroes.

It was all just a matter of time.

Timing is far more important than what most people think.

I sipped on my tropical fruit juice and thought hard about the twins, then I thought about Betty, and the four guys she was picking up.

The Fuzz Cats.

What the hell is a Fuzz Cat anyway?

If you thought the Paradox Twins were freaky, wait till you hear about these guys.

CHAPTER 12

THE FUZZ CATS

"I wonder how Betty's getting on?" I asked. "Oh, I'm sure she's all right, she's probably on her way back with The Fuzzy Fuzz Cats by now."

"What exactly is a Fuzz Cat, Sasha?" I was dying to know.

"Follow me up to the roof terrace and I'll tell you all about them. I need to pop into the greenhouse, to pick some more herbs for the pasta sauce."

"Sure, ok," I said. So, up to the roof terrace we went, spending just two minutes in the greenhouse we walked back out and parked our bums on the old wooden picnic bench. "Hey let's stay up here for a while, it's really nice out today." I agreed. The weather was perfect, we had naked sacred blue skies above us, fresh-sexy-crispy sunshine, ha! "Ok, so now I will tell you all about The Fuzz Cats. The Fuzz Cats are four brothers who grew up in East London, their names are Bruce, Brian, Sam and George. Their dad's name is JJ, and their mum's name is Rose, Rose makes the best cup of tea in London, by the way."

Sasha reached forward to open the big red and white stripy umbrella, we urgently needed shade from the blazing hot Italiano sunshine, the soft passing breeze made the bright brolly spin wildly, like an old-fashioned merry-go-round. Sasha swiftly slipped back into his delightful story-telling voice, he was quite charming.

"Ok, so…The Fuzzies. Now, these four brothers all used to be normal teenage kids, that was back when they all lived at home, and worked hard for their dad, in the family business – they had a small household removal firm you see. Every morning they drove to the yard, hopped-up in their big old removal truck, and zoomed off out to work, it wasn't rocket science, it was straight-forward donkey work, lots of 'lifting and shifting,' they simply moved families, with all their gear, from one house to another." Sasha suddenly stopped himself.

"Oh, pants! Sorry Louise, I almost forgot. I need to pop downstairs to quickly put these herbs in the pasta sauce, I'll be back in a jiffy." Sasha shot downstairs and made it back up to the roof terrace in under ninety seconds. He was fast and silent, like a ninja-librarian. "Ok, so now I will tell you how these four hard-working brothers got transformed into The Fuzz Cats. It all happened in late September, back in 1966. There's a black cat involved in this story too, his name is Mungo. I think I will tell you about him first." Sasha smiled, he liked company. "Old Mungo belonged to Roaring Meg, the crazy psycho. He was quite a boring old cat, pretty dull, stupid and lazy. Now, wherever Meg went, Mungo the knit-wit-twitty-kit-cat followed, this crossed-eyed docile furry dip-stick had a very unenthusiastic brain, he looked quite demented. Now, unfortunately, Meg's drinking made a turn for the worse in

1966. She had far too much time on her hands; she was basically bored out of her knickers, ha-ha!" Sasha giggled loudly, under the shade of the umbrella.

"Meg never owned a black flying surfboard in '66, she was a more traditional 'Sixties-Witch' back then, she flew about on an old broomstick, with dopey old Mungo clinging-on to the twiggy bristles behind."

"Meg's black flying surfboard came along many years later, it was created in 1991, by a groovy-surfing-Californian-beachbum-professor called Vince, but that's another story. From 64 to 66, Meg's relationship with the booze kind of fell into a dark, sinister tunnel, she drank four bottles of whiskey every day, she was slowly turning into a fat pointless morbid blob of bad energy, he body was filled with pimple pus and bad habits. Her most dangerous habit was flying while drinking and smoking-cigars. She'd hit the skies at night when she was completely blotto, she crashed into many buildings, these wild drunk flights scared the bejesus out of poor Mungo. He was a total thick-O, but he still had feelings." Sasha giggled 'off the cuff' quite a bit, he made me laugh too.

"Another unpleasant habit Meg developed over the years was eating pigeons." Sasha sarcastically closed his eyes tight, opened his mouth, and placed two fingers on his tongue, pretending that he was gonna puke any second. Removing his fingers, he picked his nose and said,

"One Sunday afternoon, the four brothers were hanging out down at the Hackney Marshes, just playing a bit of football. Well, little did they know that Roaring Meg was flying high above them, she was on a drunken rampage, chasing down a poor old pigeon for lunch. Mungo was up there too, clinging on to the back of Meg's broomstick."

"The panicking pigeon tried his very best to keep away from Meg's hungry mouth. Flippin' and flappin' all over the place he suddenly performed a spectacular nosedive into a grove of trees, and trying his best to stay alive, the pigeon slipped a quick, slick double-kick-back-flip, but Meg was already waiting right behind him. She anticipated the pigeon's move and snatched him right out of the air, and one second later she bit his head-off!"

"Mama Mia, that's disgusting!" I said.

"I know, witches eat anything, they're pigs." He went on,

"Ok, let me tell you what happened to Mungo. When the pigeon was halfway through the double-kick-back-flip, Meg moved faster than Bruce Lee to catch the poor bird off-guard, but old Mungo wasn't ready for this sharp move, and as a result, he slipped, lost his grip and crash-landed into some trees below. The silly cat ended up head-butting a massive oak tree, he was totally out for the count." Sasha was laughing again, his scratchy 'Muttley-giggle' got me every time, ha-ha! He rambled on,

"This catty collision made a huge THUD-sound. Mungo blurted out the shortest loudest 'meow' in cat history, landing face down on the grass, he looked like a dead cat sunbathing the afternoon away. Meg knew nothing about this of course, she was busy ripping the pigeon's body to shreds, she thought Mungo was still riding shotgun, sittin on the back burner, but he was long gone. The four brothers heard the thud and rushed over to investigate. Poor Mungo was stiff all over, he'd gone into shock, he froze up like a stuffed animal, but he was still breathing. The four brothers quickly took the dazed cat back home, and placed him in the kind nurturing care of good old mum, Rose was a real sweetheart, she nursed Mungo back to good health in no time. Hot milk with a pinch of brandy did the trick." Sasha suddenly gave me the serious eyeball again, "Now hear this Louise, back in the day, that crazy-bat witch used Mungo for magic storage, kind of like a handbag. It's simple, she stashed secret heaps of raw magic deep inside Mungo's body. Of course, Mungo was completely unaware of this. That dumb old cat had lethal amounts of witch magic sleeping deep in his veins." The sun became very intense up on the roof terrace now, Sasha turned all hot and sweaty, so much so, that he decided to have a little break, he quickly kicked his shoes and socks off, and, oh my goodness, what a fantastic stink his feet distributed! Mega-Cheesy-feet. My nose was suffering now, I boldly ordered Sasha to go dip his big stinking tootsies in the Jacuzzi; and that's exactly what he did, he soon got comfortable sitting on the edge of the tub, then he cracked on with the story. "As the weeks rolled by, Mungo slowly became the new family pet, all four brothers had grown very fond of him, and Mungo soon ended up going to work with all the guys, he was part of the gang now, he loved sitting inside the big old removal truck, he'd look out the front windscreen and wonder what adventures the day might bring. His long black tail happily whipped about as he purred in harmony with the heavy hum of the lorries engine. Then, one day, JJ and sons took on a huge removal job that would change the four boy's lives forever. They moved a rich old man from Hampstead, to the Isle of Wight. Charlie Taylor was his name, selling his detached Edwardian house to a nice Turkish family, he journeyed south, moving into a lovely beachside windmill, in a place called Sandown. Now, the coolest thing about the old house in Hampstead was the beautiful swimming pool in the back yard. On the day of the move, one of the brothers heard old Charlie say, on his mobile phone, that the Hampstead house was going to be empty for five days, before the new owners moved in. Well, well… this instantly gave the four brothers a cheeky idea, they planned a midnight break-in, just to have a free swim in the backyard, that's all." I interrupted Sasha.

"Hey, I like the sound of these guys, they're cheeky.""Yes, four cheeky raccoons, ha ha." Sasha laughed and slipped, and suddenly fell into the jacuzzi. Whoops! After taking a hot five minute dip, he stepped out and sat back at the picnic bench, his clothes were soaked. I quickly ran off to fetch a soft navy jumbo towel. Sasha was keen to get on with telling me this fuzzy story, I helped dry him off.

"The move to the Isle of Wight was a piece of cake. Arriving back in London, the boys drove straight up to the big empty house in Hampstead, climbed over the side gate and headed straight for the pool. These guys were breaking the law, but they didn't care, they just wanted to have some fun, it wasn't like they were stealing diamonds, they just wanted to have a free swim." I understood.

"Mungo wanted to have some fun too; the behaviour of that crazy cat was very surprising. Cats don't usually swim, but Mungo was the exception. Along with the four brothers, he jumped in and out of that pool all night long; they were having a blast. Then, halfway through the night, the brothers ordered themselves an extra large deep-pan Hawaiian pizza, which they scoffed-up in no time, and soon after that, the night got colder. It was already cold out, but now it was freezing, then a thunderstorm came." I quickly dashed back down into Sasha's pad, to fetch him a dry pair of jeans and a clean T shirt, I grabbed some more towels as well. He quickly got changed in the greenhouse, I decided to hang his wet clothes on the outside railing, the static around this dude was insane, Sasha has a very rich dynamite-aura buzzing all over him, it felt good being close to him, he rambled on. "The boys didn't care too much for the weather, they were too busy doing their bombs and somersaults, behaving like there was no tomorrow. Then a hard rain came crashing down, followed by endless whips of thunder and lightning dancing above. It was a fierce storm, but these young dudes were fearless. They pretended the lightning was disco lights sent from heaven above; their adrenaline ran sky high." Sasha started waving his finger at me. "Swimming in an open-air pool under a heavy thunderstorm is a very dangerous Rock n Roll thing to do Louise. So dangerous that it created a crazy life-changing moment for these young wild-cats." Sasha rapped on. "Without any warning, a huge jagged bolt of lightning stabbed its way down through the sky and hit the swimming pool with a huge whacking bazooka blast! All the boys (along with the cat) were in the water at this crucial moment. This turned out to be a fleeting mis-fit of spooky nature at its wildest - all the brothers got completely electrocuted! Mungo the cat died instantly - he got frizzle-fried down to his bones in seconds, his whole body dissolved into the electric water. Things weren't really looking much better for the boys. An unlimited amount of electricity poured its way down through the jagged bolt of lightning, and in a blink it quickly shot back up into the sky, only to come slashing back down for a second zap. Holy smoke! Things really started cooking now; strange chemicals mixed with electrical currents stirred about in the water. The witch magic stored inside Mungo's body, along with Mungo's catty DNA, swirled about in the wet swish too. The four brothers experienced some radically intense electric-shock treatment, all at an extremely high voltage, but they were still managing to stay alive, somehow." Holy Shunka-Tunka, Sasha had some crazy-poolside stories. He went on. "All the electricity circulating through the water found its way into their bones. They got wham-jolted and jam-slapped from head to toe; they looked like they were doing some kind of crazy sizzle-sneeze dance, like this." Sasha suddenly jumped-up from the bench and danced about like a crazy zombie made of jelly, he looked nuts. He jolted about anxiously, moving all wacky, like he had a hyperactive squirrel stuck in his underpants, he looked so silly, my tummy hurt from laughing, then he finally sat back down and vividly explained, "It was like the swimming pool had turned into a huge cauldron full of cosmic energy. There was a lot going on, Louise, I think everything quickly got mixed together, electricity mixed with Mungo's DNA, and witch magic mixed with freezing cold water, all these elements came together and quickly turned into one source of unique phenomenal substance. It found a new home in the hearts and veins of the four brothers. The pool was full of choppy waves and strong electrical undercurrents now, the four boys got zapped into a frenzy, ping-trotted into a deep trance, completely zing-fired and whip-slapped all over the place." Sasha became silent for a few seconds.

"Great Scott! How ever did they survive?" I asked.

"I have absolutely no idea, Lou-Bee-Lou. That is a total mystery, my love. They should have died in that pool, but some freaky supernatural miracle decided to save them. It was a huge transformation; for ten strange minutes they got slam-jammed from head to toe. It must have felt like being trapped inside a blender full of electric eels. This extremely strange event had successfully transformed these guys into THE FUZZ CATS. They shined wildly like the stars above; these electric guys were fully charged-up now. Their hairstyles looked all fuzzy and bushy, they looked a little bit like THE JACKSON 5, their fingernails turned into cat's claws, and their ears became all pointy like 'Spock.' They all seemed to be more catty and agile; sharper in their senses y'know, like wild pumas. Mungo's DNA had found its way into their flesh and bones, and as a bonus, these Cat-boys absorbed all the witch magic too, all this got mixed with the electricity in their veins. This was nuts! Every brother now had a brand new
'super-unique' electric power living inside them."

The Fuzz Cats

"They knew it was their duty to develop their magically-driven skills, it was all a matter of patience and practice, lots of repetition. Well, I'm pleased to say that they've come a long way, Louise. They use their powers very wisely these days, they practice karate, kung-fu, and all that other martial arts stuff. They even meditate on Sundays." I sat back, put my hand on my head, and sighed a big sigh. "Well, blow me down, Sasha. These guys sound like they're the coolest cats in town."

"Yes, they are, ha-ha!" Sasha stretched his arms right out,

he quickly stood up and danced about like Fred Astaire.

"I'm popping back down to the kitchen now, I need to check up on all the food." He quickly ran off, but he was back after three minutes, with two big glasses full of coconut juice, he rambled on some more.

"From that day on, the four brothers were never the same. There's no turning back for these guys now. They're going to be The Fuzz Cats for the rest of their lives, which is pretty cool because they have now grown into the role of behaving like secret underground heroes, they could easily be described as human mobile power stations, they live in a very high vibration of pure electric joy, they never get tired, their energy readings go right off the charts, and they love listening to a band called, THE KINKS." A very cool band. "These guys live in a big warehouse in East London. It's in a very remote area, where nobody disturbs them, and that's just the way they like it. They only come out at night, in a big old ice cream van. They fight crime and help homeless people. In the winter months they hand out soup to the homeless, and in the summer months they hand out cherry-flavoured ice cold smoothies." Cherry-flavoured smoothies, oh la-la, I bet they taste nice. "Over the years, they've become highly skilled in sword fighting, Jui Jitzu and Aikido. Supersonic-secret-guardian-ninja-angels of the night, they've helped so many people, all on the sly, y'know."

"If, for example, a man coming home late after work got jumped by a gang of angry thugs, The Fuzz Cats would intervene and protect the man. They'd make sure he got home safely with his wallet, phone and credit cards, but they'd also help the thugs; they'd give 'em money and books to read. The book they love to give away most is; 'The Power of Your Subconscious Mind' by Dr Joseph Murphy. The Fuzz Cats want to help everyone, Louise."

"Hey that's really cool, Sasha."

I wasn't being cheeky or sarcastic, I meant it, sincerely.

We both sat back and sipped on our coconut juice, and after taking a big fat gulp, Sasha said, "So, now you know a little bit about The Fuzz Cats and The Paradox Twins," he smiled like Gene Kelly again. I didn't know what to say, I stood and raised my glass high, like a happy bingo winner, "Sasha, it's a pleasure knowing you my friend, we only met yesterday but it already feels like ten years, and I look forward to meeting every single member of our new tenacious gang tonight." I was very happy to be in the presence of such a fine wizard. I felt safe with Sonic Sasha, he spoke from the heart. We clinked our glasses.

"Oh, I forget to tell you – sometimes The Fuzz Cats leave their ice cream van at home, and go out on their skateboards instead, they usually do this in the summer. And sometimes they secretly go to Bournemouth, to surf under the moon, around two am. They love doing that."

CHAPTER 13

KELLY ANN

We had a nice light lunch on the roof terrace that afternoon: Parma ham with fresh melon, and after we ate, I saw an expression on Sasha's face that I hadn't seen before, he suddenly looked quite emotional about something, but this time, it was more of a sad feeling.

This was going to be interesting, I thought to myself.

We both made our way back down towards the kitchen, and while walking through the cosy restaurant area, I intuitively felt that it was just a matter of seconds before Sasha turned around to tell me that he had something new to say.

"Louise, I have something else to say, something new."

See, I told you. Sasha decided to drop a news bomb on me, he wanted to tell me all about his other beautiful daughter, a wonderful sweet girl who lives right in the heart of Camden Town, back over in north London.

"Louise, I would like to tell you all about my younger daughter, Kelly Ann, she's an eccentric water gipsy, living inside an old-fashioned Dutch barge, situated on the canal, right by Camden market. Kelly is a lovely sensitive girl, she has light purple hair and wears dark purple lipstick, she's got a lovely beauty spot right on the tip of her nose, and she sleeps peacefully on the still waters of the canal every night. Some folks call her 'Little Wing,' because she loves Jimi Hendrix, but I think she's more like 'Cynthia Rose' the strange girl from that 'Prince' song, 'Starfish and Coffee.' Or maybe 'Suzanne' by Leonard Cohen. She works two minutes from home, selling saxophones and roller-skates in Camden market, except on Sundays, when she works in the art gallery, up at the stables." Cor Blimey Guv, sounds like I have another weirdo to get acquainted with. There was a pretty big spark burning in Sasha's heart when he spoke about Kelly.

"Kelly keeps busy most evenings, if it rains, she'll stay home and watch movies while making jewellery, but if it's warm and dry out, she helps organise illegal races for quirky old wrinkly people who love racing their electric-powered motor scooters through the back streets of Camden, they love misbehaving cos it makes them feel young again, they're all fans of the fast and furious films. Kelly also teaches lots of old people how to knit, *her* knitting circle is a far cry from a plain old boring oldies club, you wont find old farting folks sipping tea, eating biscuits and talking about the good old days, oh no. Kelly combines her knitting lessons with martial arts. Kung-Fu knitting is a very useful skill for old pensioners to master. She helps old grannies become more self-sufficient. If any young bad boys try to steal their purse, they get their butt kicked, kung-fu style." Sasha silently put both his hands together, and like Bruce Lee, he bowed gracefully. "Kelly loves making strawberry tarts, she's also a bit of a fortune teller, this comes as a natural talent when you're a telepathic Pisces dimension skipper, sometimes she talks to ghosts, but only the friendly ones. She loves blowing on her own personal saxophone while roller-skating through Camden High Street, but what she absolutely loves, above all else, is looking out for old people, she adores them, this is her calling." A few tears fell from Sasha's eyes, I watched them swiftly roll up to his hairline.

"She sounds like a great kid, Sasha, a real fireball. Gosh, I'm really looking forward to meeting her." I smiled again.

She sounded like a bowl of cherries when you compare her to The Fuzz Cats and The Paradox Twins.

Sniffling away, Sasha nodded to me in agreement.

"Yes, she is lovely, I know I'm biased, cos I'm her father, I just think she's wonderful, and ridiculously beautiful."

Sasha was terribly proud of both his lovely daughters, but he was angry at himself, for being such an absent father.

"She'll definitely be here tonight, Louise. I just know it. Kelly Ann feels everything! I believe it's a gift you know. She knows we're all meeting up, over here in Italia, she picks up feelings like a vacuum cleaner picks up dust."

"She doesn't have a mobile phone, she never spends time on social media, and she hardly ever watches any TV. She prefers doing things the old-fashioned way, y'know, like talking and laughing with friends, face to face."

"She really enjoys chatting with her pals in the market, and she absolutely loves handing out free cupcakes, and free pieces of home-made jewellery. Most of Kelly Ann's customers end up becoming casual friends. She wins them over 'cos she constantly wears her heart on her sleeve, this is probably because of her weird family background. Some folks close up, while others keep an open heart, Kelly pretty much connects with everyone."
Sasha knew an awful lot about Kelly Ann, maybe he went to Camden to secretly spy on her from time to time. He had so much love for his daughters. Under all the weird mystical wizard stuff, he was just a typical doting father, full of love and longing. He went on,
"She's always got a good book on the go."
"She's read all of Roald Dahl's books, and JRR Tolkien,

and she loves all the Harry Potter books, she's read all of them six times over. Kelly finds it quite hard to fit in. She can't believe the way so many people have their faces stuck to their phones all day long, and deep down, I think she finds it hard to accept that she's the daughter of a wizard. She gets frustrated because she has great powers, but nobody has ever taught her how to use them effectively." I listened intensely. It was plain to see that Sasha was disturbed by his failures. He passionately wanted to be closer to both his daughters, determined to be a better father, but the difficult circumstances of being a maverick wizard wanted by a psycho-fudge-brain-witch-woman kept them apart. He went on.

"Kelly's telepathy is ultra sensitive, I guarantee she'll be here tonight, she knows her presence is requested."

Sasha suddenly broke down in tears, he cried and cried, just like a little boy; it was very endearing. He did that silly thing that so many folks do when they're having a sob, he tried to cry and talk at the same time. Oh dear, I was trying my best not to laugh; I just about understood his mumbling words. Wiping his dribble away, he rambled on,

"Every morning, just before she sets off to work, Kelly puts a fresh red rose in her hair. She has such a busy and extraordinary life. I love her so much, Louise. I hope she isn't lonely, maybe she has a nice boyfriend now? I hope so. She's so pretty." Poor

Sasha, he really missed his girls. I just listened away like a therapist - listen, listen, listen… without judgement, let the wizard ramble on some more.

"I guess you could say she's a bit of a genius, she seems to know a little bit about everything. She's become a super fast reader, she used to be dyslexic, but she just kept reading, and more brain cells grew in her head, making her dyslexia slowly fade away, it's still there, but it's much weaker these days." Sasha smiled like Mona Lisa.

"She probably knows all about this new tenacious gang. Premonitions come to her mind all day long. She always knew I was here, hiding out in Italy, I wanted her to come visit but it just wasn't on the cards, she couldn't whisper a word to anyone, not even Betty. That must have been such a drag. Poor Kelly, she has found it so hard to be happy, knowing I was alive, and having to stay away for so long; it's just not fair. That's a heavy burden for any daughter to carry, I wish I could go back and change things." Oh Sasha, I was seeing a whole new side to this emotional wizard. I reached up to give him the biggest hug I could manage. Under all this grief I reckon he was just a bit nervous, quite soon he was going to be in the presence of both his daughters, and when was that last time that happened, I wonder? All three of them together, having a fine meal at the table, accompanied by a big bunch of dangerous dandelion freaks, ha! I was nervous too, I kept thinking about Leon and

Tigerlips, and those electric Fuzz Cats. They all seemed to be so twisted and bizarre. I was scared in my mind, but excited in my heart. Deep down inside, I was kind of looking forward to being in their presence. After ten more minutes, Sasha finally started pulling himself back together. I grabbed a few pieces of fresh kitchen roll and handed them up to him, he was such a cry-baby, it was all quite unexpected, seeing this side of Sasha.

Once he wiped his sniffles away, I asked him to stoop down to my level, I pretended that I had something important to tell him, but I actually just wanted to give him a big sloppy kiss on the side of his cheek. I did just that, and he was pleasantly surprised, I threw a big loving smile into his dreamy eyes, and quickly followed this-up by giving him a soft cheeky slap on the face,"Cheer up, Guvnor!" I said. "Take a look on the bright side of things, we're all still alive, and the best is yet to come." My lively spirit seemed to reach Sasha, it perked him back up in two seconds. It was quite endearing seeing a fully-grown man expressing his feelings like this. In just three minutes, Sasha's soul jumped back into it's usual optimistic quirky disposition, he was feeling right as rain, singing and whistling along to the radio again. His resilient 'bounce-back-ability' was pretty sharp and healthy. And do you know what…That's exactly how we all need to be in this crazy old world… We need to stay sharp and think healthy, bounce back up, and keep smiling. Amen to that.

CHAPTER 14

HERE COMES THE COSMIC CAVALRY

Sasha had a nice little job for me now, he wanted me to re-arrange all the chairs and tables in the restaurant area, not the biggest challenge in the world. "Just shove them all together please, Louise, make one big Ma-hoo-sive table in the middle, ok honey." Sasha sprinted back into the kitchen, to keep an eye on all the food, then suddenly, at the top of his voice I heard him say… "MA-HOOOOO-SIVE!" One mahoosive table coming up, I whispered to myself. I set everything up with a huge smile on my face, this was easy work, I wanted the ma-hoo-sive table to be close to the big open log fire. Man, I love that fire! It's the heart of the house. I put three sunflowers in a vase, and placed them bang in the middle of the grand table, Sasha waltzed back in to inspect my work. "Excellent job, Louise, make sure there's lots of cutlery and plates and glasses laid out please." I took care of everything, then I suddenly heard some childish lullaby music, I think it was the 'Yankee Doodle' nursery rhyme song, it was blasting out from an old speaker that was attached to a vintage 70's ice cream van, I then heard the bold sound of Betty's jet-powered rocket ironing board, and a motorbike revving away. Half a second later Max Redwood zoomed-in through the window, and like a crazy wasp he swished through the flames of the open fire, he landed on my blue head for a second, but he soon took off again, only to land on Sasha's shoulder. He was a dashing robin. "Hey, he likes you," said Sasha, he dug into his pocket and pulled out some bird seed for Max to nibble through. I spoke up,

"Sounds like everyone's arriving back at the same time."

"Well, that's just groovy, baby," I think Sasha was more focused on having all the food ready in time. I was eager to catch a glimpse of our fantastic guests. I rushed over to the window and gazed down like an obsessed fan, I was so excited. Sasha walked over and stood calmly beside me, he leaned out the window and gently spoke up, "Come upstairs, everyone. Dinner will be served in ten minutes." Looking down towards the crowded cafe entrance, I suddenly became over-thrilled to see all these unique characters. Every word Sasha said in his descriptive story-telling tales turned out to be true. It looked like a 'Trick or Treat' Halloween freak-fest down there. I saw The Fuzz Cats hop out their ice cream van, Wow! They looked like spooky rock-star legends. Then I saw The Paradox Twins riding their fancy 'IRON JOHN' flying motorbike. Leon, the cool vampire wolf man wore a black leather jacket, with black biker's goggles, he had wavy hair and no crash helmet, his fangs looked terribly sharp. Then I saw Tigerlips, the electric eccentric stingray Tiger-man, I watched him slowly climb out of the side-car. Holy smoke, he looked so cool, he had such a fierce smile. He moved like a tiger at first, but he soon stood up and walked just like a man, he had a black leather jacket on too; it was all scratched-up and worn out. These two dudes looked like shabby old retired Hollywood stuntmen, they could have been the star attraction at a mad circus, or ghouls from Michael Jackson's 'Thriller' video…the same goes for The Fuzz Cats. I couldn't believe I was going to have dinner with all these magnificent mavericks. It was like they all jumped out from the pages of a haunted comic book; they looked like a bunch of fantastically messed-up zombie-mongrels. Hey, another vehicle suddenly pulled up – it was the washing machine 'spinner.' I noticed the driver had light purple hair. That's got to be Kelly Ann, I whispered to myself. I continued gazing down like a wise silent owl, just watching everything with my mouth wide open. I was awestruck with delight; this was an amazing gathering. I watched Betty and Kelly greet each other with a big loving sisterly hug, I heard Kelly Ann say…

"Hey Sis, I hope you don't mind me taking the spinner out for a drive. I needed to get out here fast!" Betty gave Kelly another big hug.

"Oh honey, of course I don't mind. It's just so nice to see you! I've missed my little Sis." Kelly Ann smiled brightly. Sasha was right, she was so damn pretty. Both his girls were absolute stunners, sweet eccentric angel-chicks. Shuffling into the coffee shop one by one, everyone slowly made their way upstairs. Trying ever so hard not to stare, I watched every single gang member walk into the restaurant area, moving with wary alertness, they all gravitated towards the grand Ma-Hoo-Sive table, it took about ten minutes for everyone to finally sit down. Sasha was overjoyed to have everyone there, he gave Kelly the biggest longest hug ever, many tears flowed up. The energy in the restaurant was so powerful, my rib twitched and glowed under my t-shirt like crazy, dinner time was just minutes away now. My heart suddenly tapped into a deep happiness within, this unique event truly was a special gathering, what a privilege it was to be so close to all these rare spirits, I felt like I was a million miles away from my old lonely self. The big thing that turned me on was the overwhelming flow of honesty in the room. I know some of the gang were damaged souls, but that didn't really matter all that much, the vibration of robust heart energy around that table was dynamic, undeniable and uncompromising. Sasha's overspilling aura lifted everyone up into a vibe of bold unconditional love. These guys had all been called up by Mr Sonic, and they all responded, turning up with a stout willing heart, like Ronin Samurai soldiers, and you can't ask for more than that can you? I liked being around these guys and girls, it felt good, damn good. Any blind person would know exactly what I was talking about here, they'd catch my drift in seconds, it was all about the vibe, this gang had an amazing vibe, it was positive, rich and thick, a bit like a Beatles song, 'Help' is my favourite. We all need help from time to time. I think blind individuals feel things more intensely than every-day people y'know. They pick up 'kind-hearted-energy' with their senses, my grandmother Doris was blind, she got hit by a bus.

I tell you now, this new gang, forming right in front of me was a universe away from being normal, ha-ha! I love it.

I fitted right in, it felt like I had finally found my clan.

Anyway, who wants to be normal? Not me.

Being normal sounds like a curse.

BE WHO YOU REALLY WANT TO BE, that's the best advice anyone can give, or receive.

I'm sure you understand.

I bet you have a good sharp brain sitting between your ears.

I know you have good taste,

Well, you must do,

you're reading my book,

ha-ha.

Let's eat.

CHAPTER 15

A TENACIOUS GANG IS FORMED

Old Leon the wolf-man had quite a stink on him, so I opened some windows, there was a variety of different emotions lingering about in the restaurant that night, lots of gritty, scratchy, damaged feelings in the air. To put in bluntly, it felt like RAW LOVE mixed with a sprinkle of PAIN. All of us huddled together in one room seemed to create a crazy mixture of snappy electrical energy. This bulging mass of invisible emotional content made the log fire roar up in glory, it took quite a while for the flames to calm back down, things slowly became more peaceful, and interesting. Our new guests were slowly letting their guards down; it's not easy for tough warriors to come out from behind their walls of invisible armour. Many rugged souls out there have spent years developing 'thick-skin,' as a means of protection and survival, it doesn't come natural to just let it all go and be vulnerable at dinner time, but saying that, there was a shift of energy in the room, maybe it was LOVE slowly thawing the numbness away. I started creating a list in my mind, a detailed focus on all the different powers we had among us: there was wizard magic, vampire-wolf powers, psychic mind powers, purple magic, witch powers, and a wonderful kind of electrical-cat-energy in the air. I think the purple magic was the strongest. I only say this because my rib throbbed like I had two hearts beating under my chest – all this magical energy crammed into one room was overwhelming, but I liked it, a lot. The Fuzz Cats seemed to buzz loudly, like one of those outdoor electrical lamps, y'know the ones that kill bugs, they sounded snappy and whippy. Tiger had quite a buzzy aura around him too, sitting next to The Fuzz Cats gave him electrostatic hair, it stretched up high, like it was reaching for the stars. Tiger and The Fuzz Cats became good buddies immediately, all the electricity in their bloodstream allowed them to function on the same frequency level. I suddenly noticed how Kelly Ann couldn't keep her eyes off the handsome Tiger-man, perhaps there was some 'romantic electricity' in the air as well, ha-ha.

Leon, the wolf man, was pretty quiet at the table. He struck me as the strong silent type; he seemed to be completely unafraid of everything. He stared at me across the Ma-Hoo-Sive table for five minutes straight, not batting an eyelid once; intimidating but quite impressive. His curious blue eyes were extremely cold-looking, deeply mysterious, I wondered what was going on behind them? Maybe he was thinking about eating me? I took a gamble and stuck my tongue out at him, just to try and make him smile, but all he did was raise his eyebrows. His face looked so damn spooky. Just to be kind, I decided to put a sunflower in front of him, and he flippin ate it. Haha! Nice.

Leon had the serious focus of a professional chess player.

Betty and Kelly chatted away endlessly about skin creams and hair dye. Kelly said she was thinking about changing her purple hair to a light green 'Aqua mermaid' shade, or maybe the 'Dark Green Seaweed' look, I liked it as it was, purple looked perfect on her. Now stroking my blue hair Betty expressed fervently how she loved the 'sky blue' effect – just girly talk I guess. Hanging out with this crew was fun. It was time for all these individuals to come together and work as a team. Sasha had a lot of faith in us; he was slowly injecting a brand new 'teamwork spirit' into our hearts. I trusted Sasha – he knew how to get things done, he knew exactly how to get tip-top-flip-flop relaxed confident results, he was a calm peaceful man. Sasha clapped his hands twice with authority, and everyone hushed-down and sat-up. No hang on, they sat-down and hushed-up. Dinner time had finally arrived. Yes! I was absolutely starving. Using a pinch of purple magic, Sasha flew all the food out of the kitchen and into the restaurant, the plates and bowls hovered along in single-file, floating lightly like a train of yummy international cuisines, landing gracefully on the ma-hoo-sive dinner table. On a huge silver tray Max Redwood brought out serviettes, salt and pepper pots, horseradish, mint sauce, wholegrain mustard, cranberry sauce, rainbow pepper, and beef gravy, he balanced the posh tray perfectly on his little robin head. The table was covered with delicious treats now. It was a beautifully displayed banquet. We had Sasha's magnificent banana-beef lasagne, his freshly-made penne pasta with pesto sauce, his world-famous wiggly spaghetti bolognese, served in a delightful tangy spicy herb sauce, we had smoked salmon served on thin slices of French baguette bread. We had bangers and meatballs served with cauliflower and broccoli, all cooked in soft stinky cheese, (the bangers and meatballs weren't the exploding kind…phew), we had big fat chips all covered in ketchup, served in a massive wooden fruit bowl, they were perfect. On the other side of the table was a huge salad bowl full of hot puffy chips soaked in barbecue sauce, Leon ate all of them, Pig! We had Parmesan cheese, fresh olive oil to dip our bread into. We had a big pizza to share, we had balsamic vinegar, lots of green olives, strawberry-flavoured jelly, raspberry-flavoured ice cream, cinnamon bird seed for Max, sea mussels and squid soup for Tiger, lots of coconut-flavoured smoothies, a delicious mango and blueberry fruit salad, a huge jug of carrot juice (Leon the wolf-pig drank all of it), and a huge salad, the salad dressing was a minty sauce topped with a touch of ginger, very tasty. We all stared at Sasha like patient obedient labradors, just waiting for our gang leader to give us the green-light-go-ahead. On your marks, set, get ready…Sasha waited sixty seconds, just enough time for all the rich aromas to get up our nostrils, he finally spoke…"OK, let's eat!" And we all dived into the magnificent feast before us.

After seven minutes of munching and scoffing, everyone seemed to be more relaxed and happy; the fantastic food inside us made ALL the difference. Lots of light-hearted conversation suddenly kicked off. All the gang were slowly breaking the walls down - talking about the weather, or how fast their vehicles could travel - and shortly after that everyone started to compliment Sasha on cooking such a fine feast. Sasha stood-up and bowed gracefully; he hardly said a word, he knew it was too early in the evening to start going on about his big plans, he kept himself busy making sure everyone felt at home - he was a good host, old fashioned ways are the best, he knew full well that everybody needed a good gut-full of real authentic food before anything else. He boldly ordered all of us to chew slowly. All was going nice and smooth, when suddenly, out of the blue, we got a nice surprise presented to us, Kelly Ann stood up to make a freaky announcement.

"Listen up, guys, I need to tell y'all something - we have a spirit here among us." All the chewing and chatting suddenly stopped. What the hell was Kelly going on about? The brand new silence in the air suggested that the whole gang was keen to hear what this pretty young lady had to say. I suddenly noticed how Tigerlips enjoyed gazing at Kelly's face, just as much as she enjoyed gazing at his. Everyone in the gang was curious, even Sasha. The fire crackled loudly as Kelly unravelled what she felt.

"It's nothing to worry about, I just wanted to let you guys know that we have a visitor… a ghost has joined us for dinner, she's a tough old girl, and she wants to be part of this gang. She has a good heart and a strong spirit. Her name is Penelope Jones, she was once a famous boxer, back in North London." Oh my goodness, I couldn't believe my ears. My mum used to tell me bedtime stories about the legendary Penelope Jones, when I was six years old. Miss Jones was an infamous crazy-mama! An illegal female boxer, she was a wild turkey back in the early 1920's, and now I get to meet her ghost, this was insane! Sasha got everyone to shuffle round the table, we had to make room for one more spooky ghost guest.

"Can somebody go grab another chair please," asked Sasha. I was happy to do this. I quickly found a spare chair and pushed it in towards the table, and there she was, Penelope Jones suddenly appeared, sitting comfortably right in front of me. She was as light as a feather - a featherweight, haha. She wore a mustard yellow silky boxer's gown, she had her nick-name written in fancy black embroidered letters across the back.

BONE-SHAKER-JONES! She sure was a beefy old girl, butch and bulky, but very light on her feet, she danced around like the great Muhammad Ali.

Penelope's wrinkly old face reminded me of a walnut shell. I reached over to touch her boxing gloves, but my hands went straight through them.

"Ahh-ha... I'm a ghost, my dear, you can't touch me." Penelope suddenly stood up and started dancing about like a rapper called MC Hammer, she kept saying the same words over and over, "U can't touch this."

She bopped up and down as she punched and jabbed the air in front of her. She was a fun-loving cheeky old gal, I found her to be very likeable. Oh I say, looks like we have another black-sheep-weirdo joining the gang, she spoke,

"I think you guys are alright, and I wanna help y'all."

Her earnest willing spirit was vivacious and endearing.

Sasha suddenly filled the room up with his deep 'lion-like' voice, "Yes, Ok, that's lovely. Thank you Penelope, we're very happy to have you with us. Right, so, it looks like we're all here now." Sasha poured some red grape juice into his glass; it looked like red wine." Now, before I tell you all about my masterplan, I want to express that I completely disagree with violence." What!?

Everyone looked at each other in shock. Sasha continued.

"I know it's going to get ugly, hairy and crazy when the awful witch army comes down from the moon, but if we go to war with them, it will just be madness. There's nothing good about violence and war and killing; It's all stupid. Being violent is choosing to live at the lowest level of intelligence; in fact, it's beneath intelligence." Penelope spoke out some more, "I agree, I think we all need to be more like Gandhi. I was violent in the ring for almost all my life, and it messed me up big-time! I ended up getting arthritis in both my hands. I'm dead now, but my knobbly knees still rattle like crazy, I never got to be old and happy, violence screwed me right up. Some mornings I punched the postman, just because I didn't like the song he was singing, I had lots of issues, and I died at the age of forty-nine, that's so young. I should have been a race-car driver, or a river dancer, if I had a more peaceful life, I bet I would have lived longer." Penelope started to do the river dance, she was a dotty old fruit loop cracker-jack sweetheart.

Sasha raised his right hand to gently encourage Penelope to button it, hush-up old girl. Now sitting back in his chair, he took a quick sip on his grape juice before ordering Max to dim the lights, we were eating in the dark now. The fire suddenly looked a bit too mellow, lots of embers but no flames, I went to throw some more wood on, but Betty beat me to it, she reached over and quickly chucked two logs into the hearth, there was a dirty old wine barrel in the corner, it was full of logs and kindling, Max topped-it up every day. God I love that fire, it's so beautiful and relaxing. I could watch it for hours, just sitting there, listening to the crackles, while reading a good book, that would be utterly divine. Sasha's strong presence and calming aura silently won the trust and attention of the whole gang. In five seconds everyone simmered down, we were waiting for Sasha to begin, it was time for our captain to reveal his masterplan. Now, I won't be giving much away on Sasha's sensational masterplan, cos where's the fun in that? Anyway, the old wizard only wanted to reveal little segments at a time. He was quite a secretive guy. What I will tell you is this… Sasha's intentions were very good, so good that he had no desire to kill Roaring Meg, or any of the mini witches for that matter. He wanted to turn the tables on everything. His plan was quite weird, and pretty surprising, but then again, so is Sasha.

So, Nik-Nak-Paddy-Wak, you better read on.

CHAPTER 16

ONE POWERFUL HEART VISIT

The first stage of Sasha's masterplan included one of his favourite spells. I'm talking about the famous HEART VISIT SPELL. Do you know it? When I first heard about this spell I thought it was a load of horse manure, but my attitude changed when Sasha explained things in greater depth, and more detail.

The heart visit spell takes place when a wizard, like Sasha, turns himself into a spirit and pays a little visit to someone's heart, with the sole desire to give them strength and hope. He might stay inside someone's heart for a couple of days, but if they're going through a really tough patch, he'll stay longer. I know this to be true because Sonic Sasha stayed in my heart for two weeks, just after my folks disappeared. I knew nothing about this of course, till recently, but looking back, I must say, it did feel like someone, or something was helping me carry on. So, the time had come for another heart visit, but this time it was going to be far more dangerous, and way more complicated, excellent news! I love danger! Hanging out with these stardust bandits, I began to realise and accept that danger was just an everyday part of life. It kept us sharp, and on our toes. Many times, under my skin, I felt my adrenaline dance with my endorphins, just like how Torvill danced with Dean, back in the

84 Winter Olympics. Jumping into a daring complex heart visit was going to be dicey, the whole gang were coming along for the ride on this one, this had never been done before, the outcome could land anywhere between magnificent and catastrophic. I was curious to know whose heart we were going to visit, and why? What I'm about to say now won't make much sense, but it will in time, so just bear with me. Sasha wanted the whole gang to work as a team, he wanted us to pick the Titanic shipwreck up from the bottom of the ocean, and take it over to Hudson Bay, in Canada. The Titanic had been resting on the Atlantic seabed ever since it sank, back in 1912, on the 15th April, just hours after hitting the iceberg. It would take a great deal of strength and stamina to pick this old baby up. Sasha's mad plan was a twisted stroke of genius, he believed we could pull it off, and after a while, I started to believe it too. Sasha boldly announced the heart we were going to visit. "Ok, guys, we're all going to climb into the mighty passionate heart of Max Redwood - the Magnificent Robin." The whole gang roared with great laughter, it felt like we were in a rowdy pub now. I mean really, come on Sasha, how can a wizard pull a stunt like that? The whole gang fitting inside the tiny heart of Max Redwood, it sounds bonkers, it makes no sense at all, but sometimes that's exactly how wizard magic works, it looks mental and potty at first, but in the end it all comes out wickedly

cool. When the laughter finally fizzled out, an air of seriousness filled the restaurant, everyone soon began to realise, and slowly accept, that Sonic Sasha meant business, this cosmic sky-cat was sticking to his guns. He was in a very intense mood, maybe he was a Scorpio? He quickly pointed out that he wanted brave little me to be part of this mission, we needed all the purple magic we could get our hands on, my new rib pushed lots of purple magic through my veins, I was happy to help, I would have been bored out of my socks if they left me here to clean up and wash all the dishes, sod that for a laugh. Everyone was game, ultra keen to get a move on, Sasha closed his eyes, put his hands together and slowly turned the whole gang into smokey spirits, and soon after, he turned us into one big giant puff of fog, this felt so weird, but only for a few minutes. The strength of The Paradox Twins, The Fuzz Cats, Penelope Jones, Sonic Sasha, Betty and Kelly Ann were all about to come together in one little robin heart. I felt nervous for Max, this overload of majestic power might make his body explode. Whistling out some high-pitched-melodies, Max confidently showed great enthusiasm as he leaned forward to slowly inhale us, he sucked the whole gang in through his tiny little beak, his little red scarlet chest was all puffed up, we slipped down his throat and tried to get comfortable inside his delicate little body, Holy-Moly, there was no turning back now. What happened next was very surreal! Did Max turn into a huge giant-sized-robin? No. His appearance didn't change at all, but on the inside, it was a totally different story, Max suddenly turned into the world's strongest creature of ALL time! It was like he had the strength of a million stallions. This experience was the most powerful and beautiful feeling I had ever felt. Max darted out the cafe's front door like a cosmic sky-rocket, and shot straight up to the stars. We all stayed inside Max's little heart for approximately four hours; that was enough time to get the job done. Flying at 1,999 miles per hour, Max cut through the wind like a feathered bullet, it took us fifteen seconds to fly over the south of France, flying faster than a concord, we skimmed over the Atlantic Ocean, hovering about one meter above sea level, Max loved flirting with danger, he truly was an 'Evel-Knievel' kind of robin. It's hard to explain exactly how good it felt being inside little Max, it was such a rich feeling. He suddenly hit the brakes and nose-dived into the freezing cold sea. Oh my gosh this was such a rush! A cold 'stabby-cut-cut-feeling' ran through the whole gang. We swam straight down into the darkness, diving deeper and deeper, till we reached the seabed. Max knew exactly where to go, all his past 'purple-magic-runs' allowed him to swim with his eyes closed. It was the strangest sensation, being wrapped-up in a group-spirit, deep inside a robin's heart; Sasha had the strongest vibe. The ocean was so much colder down on the seabed, it felt like the loneliest place in the universe, it was awfully quiet down there, peaceful but very cut off. I flippin love the ocean, it truly is one of Mother Nature's greatest wonders. Here we go, Max suddenly found the shipwreck and started bashing his head right into its side, he was trying to loosen it up first. The Titanic snapped in half when it sank on that fatal night. We went for the stern end, Tiger's private living space. This old ship had been sitting in the exact same spot for over a hundred years. It wouldn't budge at all, but Max persevered, he behaved like a mentally disturbed gipsy, like a wild Spanish bull he rammed his head into the ship again and again, but it wouldn't budge. "Come on, Max," I shouted. "Give it some hardcore elbow grease, baby!" Soon everyone was yelling with me. "Yeh, come on, Max! You can do it!" Shouted Kelly Ann. This gave Max a huge boost of confidence. It gave him the crazy mojo edge he needed; teamwork is the key my friend. Teamwork puts fire into the hearts of champions, you know it's true. Max was revved-up now, he suddenly went loco! And then it happened, the old ship started to move. Yes! Max was slowly tilting the stubborn shipwreck over to one side. We heard a deep heavy 'twisted-steel' creaking sound, the ships movement free'd up thousands of trapped air bubbles, they quickly raced back up to the sea surface. The whole gang felt everything Max felt. This 'Wonder Robin' kept throwing himself into the side of the ship, again and again, like a determined little super-hero. On this day, Max had more strength than Godzilla. He was lean, mean, and quicker than Steve McQueen!

"Come on, Mad Max! Give it all you've got, my son!"

Max was totally pumped. Bossy Betty shouted at us now. "Come on, guys. This is a team effort - we're all here inside Max's heart together, so put your backs into it! Help Max out! WE ARE ALL ONE TODAY!" She yelled like Janis Joplin. Old Max continued bashing his head into the ship, then something unique happened, a mellow purple light started to reveal itself, the purple magic sleeping deep in the ships steel suddenly woke up and found its way into Max's bloodstream, this was a sweet result. After a whole lot of tugging and heaving, Max finally rolled the shipwreck over. Yes! A fleeting rainbow-shoal of multi-coloured-fish suddenly came bursting out among all the air bubbles, through Max's tiny eyes I saw pink exotic flat-fish scarper away like wavy ribbons, I saw thousands of electric blue lightning fish scatter away like broken pieces of glass, I saw a giant (long-bodied) stripy-back (yellow and black) tiger-rag-fish linger off like a lost scarf, and last out were two long wormy yellow eels; they looked like Elton John's shoelaces, or giant caterpillars with no legs. it's time to move out guys, sorry about that. They all fled in seconds, scurrying off into the darkness. The purple glow coming off the ship gave us just enough light to see what was going on down there. Now that the ship had successfully been flipped over, Max got himself ready to get the strongest grip he could manage; he positioned himself way down at the back, this was the best spot. Max pretty much 'stabbed' his tiny little robin claws into the ships rusty old body. I felt all the blood in his potent heart boil up like a furnace. GO ON MY SON! Then it happened… MAX STARTED LIFTING THE WHOLE DAMN SHIPWRECK UP TO THE TOP OF THE OCEAN! THIS WAS INSANE! ABSOLUTELY MIND-BLOWING! HOW THE HELLS BELLS DID HE DO THIS? To this day, I still don't understand what happened down there, I guess some things in life, I will never understand, and this was definitely one of those things. Sasha BELIEVED we could do it, and that was all that mattered. His faith, and power of belief was unbreakable, almost tangible. My faith in Sasha was a real, true solid thing. It was easy for me to trust him because he saved my life, without his rib, I'd be a gonna-doner kebab. Being inside Max's fantastic little heart with the whole gang is something I'll remember for the rest of my days. The feeling was sublime. We all moved that ship together with pure hearty teamwork, Yes-Sir-Ree. The combined strength of all the wondrous magic working together that day was absolutely phenomenal. I loved it. It was a magnificent day at sea. Night or day, who cares. Sasha yelled out like a loud proud American football coach, one who was completely obsessed with winning, "Come on, guys! We've got it now! Give it everything you've got Max! Come on! That's it! Let's have it! Hold on tight, feed that fire! Teamwork makes the dream work baby! Go for it Maxie, you sweet little fire-cracker!" Sasha was a great team leader. Old Max was happy with his grip, he flapped his little wings with pure robust-robin determination. Now, most robins usually zoom across the sky, carrying twigs or worms for their kids, right? But not Max Redwood, this SUPREMO HERO broke through the ocean surface with half the Titanic dangling under his busy wings. His little robin claws were super-powerful! What a diamond geezer! This tenacious gang had successfully injected ALL of their passionate raw strength into Max's heart and body. I remember how crazy it all felt, we climbed higher and higher into the cold starry sky. Everyone experienced an insane rush of adrenaline, kind of like a wild nitrous oxide boost, we were feeling it. Max sang a sweet happy beach boys melody as we flew confidently under the icy blue moon. Following orders from Sasha, we took the shipwreck directly to Hudson Bay, over in Canada; it wasn't that far away, not for a gang like ours, we got there in fifty-five minutes. Not too shabby at all, an excellent time, considering our heavy load. Flying over Eastern Canada I remember seeing Hudson Bay glimmering down below, it wasn't a full moon that night, just a crescent,

I saw it in the reflection of the bay, I remember this well, it looked so beautiful. Sasha knew exactly where he wanted the old shipwreck to go, he wanted it dropped back in the ocean, but not so deep this time, it had to stay close to the surface, just a couple of meters below sea level. Max released the shipwreck from his grip just one mile out from the Canadian shoreline, it hit the ocean with the biggest splash. This whole experience was flippin brilliant! In the name of teamwork, we did it. This was the first stage of Sasha's masterplan done and dusted - phase one accomplished, yeah baby! It was now time for us to head back to the rocky-roadside-mountain-cafe-bar, back in Italia. Now, perhaps you're wondering… why would Sasha want the remains of the Titanic moved to Hudson Bay? It's quite a peculiar task for any wizard to carry out. The answer to that question is simple my friend, it was all part of the fantastic masterplan. I will give you more details about this later, I promise, but for now, all you need to know is this, Sasha wants to get rid of Roaring Meg and all the mini witches, but he swore to himself not to kill or destroy them. Sonic Sasha functions on a very high vibration, the last thing this guy wants to do is destroy life, he's too kind, he's got a happy little hippy living in his heart. Peace-out.

CHAPTER 17
FOLLOWING ORDERS

Before heading back to Italia, Sasha had one more job in hand, he instructed his feathery little friend to yank the Titanic's huge rusty propeller off, and fly it over to London. The Titanic had three colossal propellers at the back. Sasha wanted the middle one, the one with four fins. Sasha's freaky formulas and strange strategies were kind of like getting a haircut from Edward Scissorhands, things might look weird half way through, but in the end, everything works out fine. Please keep this in mind as I unravel this unorthodox story.

Max did as he was told, he flew the propeller back to London, delivering it directly to Betty's Portobello Road laundromat, we left it by the back door, sitting in the city streets, it looked absolutely huge, but it was light as a feather in comparison to carrying half the Titanic.

"Good job, Maximilian. Pretty soon, this propeller's gonna come in very handy," Looks like Sasha had another zany idea up his sleeve. We flew back to the mountains for some coffee. All of us cooped up together inside Max's little heart turned out to be a cool way for the whole gang to create a strong bond. It felt weird, like we'd all been stuffed into a tiny wigwam. There was a team spirit among us now. I'd be happy to do another heart-visit with these guys; it was a unique experience, apart from the

stink, that was Leon. We arrived back at Sasha's cafe at half two in the morning. The cool wizard drew us out of Max's little heart with delicate skill and gentle precision. He moved fast because he had big plans that needed be carried out in a speedy fashion.
"Right, listen up everyone, we've got things to do and places to go. First off, I want Betty to make some major improvements on The Fuzz Cat's ice cream van, I have a few ideas that I want to put into action, but not just yet, we need to get back to London first." Sasha spoke fast and hard, like an American basketball coach during a seventy five second 'Time-out.'
"OK, so this is the next step… I want everyone to come back to Betty's laundromat with me, except for The Paradox Twins. I have a special job for you guys."
Sasha explained things in a blunt, direct manner.
"Leon and Tigerlips will be heading over to New Zealand, to fetch my huge supply of purple magic. I left it there many years ago – it's hidden in Jack's lighthouse, at Tuhawaiki Point, near Timaru." Sasha wanted Leon to fly his IRON JOHN motorbike, and Tiger to follow in the SPINNER. As soon as Sasha made this announcement, Betty took Tiger over to the spinner and proceeded to give him a quick run-down on how to operate all the fantastic features. Like a polite air stewardess Betty showed Tiger all the dashboard gadgets. She was sometimes serious, and sometimes light-hearted, just like her cosmic Daddio.

She pointed her slender finger over to the button board,

"Ok, Tigerlips, listen up please, when you hit this 'TURBO-WASH' button, the spinner automatically turns into a speedboat. Now, you must remember to push the button about five seconds before you hit the water, ok; you got that, Tiger-boy?" Tiger nodded and smiled.

"Yes Ma'am, I gotcha," that was all he said. Sasha spoke up some more, he gave the twins all the details they needed. "Getting over to New Zealand won't be a problem for a couple of rude-boys like you two. Jack's lighthouse is tiny, it looks like a B&B for dwarves - it's on the South Island, there's only one lighthouse at Tuhawaiki point, so it'll be easy to find." This New Zealand mission for the twins seemed simple at first mention, but if any witches learned about it, the situation could get heavy and go south. All they had to do was collect an old suitcase full of purple magic and bring it straight back to London, sounds like a simple operation, but Sasha knew the risk factor was high. Lots of mini witches will be roaming around soon, and no doubt, they'll be looking for anything suspicious. Sasha grabbed an old worldly travel map from his cafe and proceeded to show Leon the exact location of Timaru. Tiger continued getting familiar with the spinner, he'd never driven a vehicle before in his life, but he was a sharp cat, a fast learner. Sometimes, in this life, you have to pick things up fast, and just keep rolling.

Oh yes. That's how you win. Sasha had no immediate instructions for me, so I just sat back and watched everyone else for a while, that was the moment I noticed a growing sweetness between Kelly and Tiger. It was official, they both had a huge crush on each other. Hello-ello, romance between two weirdos… how lovely. Betty suddenly nudged Tiger, she wanted to tell him all about the fuel tank.

"Ok, pay attention please, when you fill her up, it's got to be non-biological powder, or liquid, ok. Whatever you do, don't use biological." Tiger nodded,

"Non-biological, ok, I got it." Tiger listened to Betty, but he wasn't really giving his full attention. His amber-gold eyes kept looking over to Kelly Ann, and she kept gazing back, smiles were exchanged - love was in the air, ha-ha. Old Betty suddenly turned into a hard-headed-bossy-hot-cross-bun-dinner-lady. She gave Tiger a swift slap on his cheek, "Hey, pay attention man! This is important stuff, Buster!" Tiger growled, and Kelly Ann giggled. Betty was in a snappy mood now, "You listen here, Ducky! You better make sure you look after my race car, ok, Tiger-pants! And try not to squash any school kids on your travels." I love Betty so much, she definitely had a bee under her bonnet. Maybe she was a tad jealous of all the luvvy-duvvy-ness? Sasha suddenly decided that he wanted someone else to go with The Paradox Twins, another gang member to help keep a sharp eye out, tweet-tweet, guess who?

"Max will be flying as blocker for you guys. He'll glide high above, keeping a bird's eye view on things, looking out for any wandering witches. Now, when you guys arrive at Tuhawaiki Point, someone will be there waiting for you, an old lighthouse lady called Jennie, please be nice and courteous to her, she's my ex-lover. She doesn't know you guys, but she knows Max very well. Once she sees little Mr Redwood, she'll be nice to all of you, I promise." Leon nodded sternly like a US marine, he knew exactly what to do, and he was ready-steady to crack-on with this long distance mission. Sasha smiled and said, "During this mission I'm calling you Broadsword and Danny-Boy." Sasha firmly patted the twins on their backs. Tigerlips smiled instantly, he was a fairly open-minded extrovert character, Leon didn't smile one bit, he was checking the oil level on his motorbike now, he was more like a closed-book-introvert-beast, it takes all kinds I guess.

So, the time had come for the gang to split up. Betty's jet powered rocket ironing board kindly provided a fantastically unique service for the rest of the gang - this amazing flying zinger was our ticket back to London. Let me explain: Betty placed the board directly under the Fuzz Cat's ice cream van, and clicking her fingers, the cool ironing board suddenly changed shape, it transformed itself into a huge 'old-school' American surfboard, it hovered obediently, waiting for further instructions from pink-head. Betty ordered her trusty sky-board to clamp itself firmly to the underbelly of the ice cream van. It wouldn't budge an inch now; it was locked-hard into a good set-position. The rocket board was now ready to carry the rest of the gang back to London, in the ice cream van. It was easily powerful enough to get the job done, driving the old van through Italy and France would have been nice, but we didn't have time to go sightseeing, a long drive through all the mountain roads would have taken up too much time - and we had lots to do, back in London.

Piling into the van we braced ourselves for another weird flight, quickly looking out the back window I saw Max and The Paradox Twins zoom off in the opposite direction. Tiger blew a swift kiss to Kelly, and she quickly blew one back, The Fuzz Cats saw this and couldn't stop giggling. Then Betty spoke up, "Oh I say, lookie-lookie-Tiger-wookiee, wham-bam Kelly Ann! She's got the hots for the Tiger Man." Sweet Kelly Ann suddenly turned a red beetroot colour, we all sniggered away, like pathetic school kids sat at the back of a bus. Kelly had the biggest smile on her face, "Oh, shut up," she said, she was blushing now, she politely kept to herself, singing and humming like a happy art student, she took out her sketching pad and doodled away, drawing all kinds of fancy artistic images, every one of them turned out to be some kind of tiger. The ice cream van was airborne now, flying high in the sky. Well bless Kelly Ann's cotton socks, she was falling in love. Amen and hallelujah to that. If anyone deserves a lucky break with love, it's got to be Kelly Ann. My gosh that girl has spent far too much time alone, reading her books and pining for love inside her dusty old Dutch barge.

We picked up more speed as we flew high above the mountain tops. The jet-powered rocket ironing board was coping with the load - no problems there. Our journey back to London was swift and smooth. We had a good laugh listening to The Fuzz Cats singing away, they provided some funny in-flight entertainment for us, they gave us numerous acapella renditions of all their favourite 'SIXTIES' songs, they sang with punchy passion.

They meowed and purred with the most excellent harmonies.

They were fantastic! They made a wonderfully unique sound.

They performed a completely original version of,

'Sunny Afternoon.'
A brilliant track by their favourite band…
'The Kinks.'

They don't make songs like that anymore.

CHAPTER 18

WORK YOUR MAGIC, BETTY

We got back to Betty's laundromat at four in the morning. The neighbourhood was awfully quiet, but not for long matey, the winds of change were blowing. We drove down the secret winding tunnel and quickly parked the ice cream van just where the spinner usually sits. As we climbed out, Sasha told Betty that he wanted the ice cream van transformed into a helicopter. What!? Sweet fuzz nuts! Looking stunned and amused, Betty raised her eyebrows, pushed her pouting lips to one side, and said with a smile, "Okey-dokey Daddio, I'm on it." Not wasting one second, Betty went straight to work on making this transformation a successful one, she needed to make a big pair of wings first, she decided to smash-up her 'Spitfire' fridge and gas cooker. Using an old sledgehammer, Betty battered the hell out of her old gas cooker, while Penelope Jones boxed the living daylights out of the old Spitfire fridge (we all helped ourselves to a slice of the delicious blueberry cheesecake, but there was no time to cook the sausages). They both smashed and bashed away like a couple of angry cave-girls. Betty needed a whole lotta workspace, so, to make the project pay off more handsomely, we decided to take the whole operation up onto the main street, we parked the ice cream van on the wide pavement, just in front of the laundromat, on Tavistock square.

It was still very early in the morning, around five a.m, sweet heavens above, we made so much noise, we woke ALL the neighbours up. With cranky voices they shouted abuse out their windows, telling us to shut up; some grouchy old woman threatened to call the police. I quickly rushed over to the bony-old-chainsmoker, and with a plastic smile I said that the ice cream van was the main attraction at a fancy art exhibition, it had to be finished and ready before nine am, cos it was going out on parade. I hated telling lies, but what could I do? Telling a fat porky pie was much easier than saying… 'Hi neighbour, guess what… thousands of horrible witches are coming to kill us soon, and we need to get ready.' That was the unfortunate truth. Roaring Meg and her witch army were coming to get us – no doubt about it. We were in a jam, a pickle, a slap and a tickle, ha-ha, we had to move fast. There was a very good reason why Sasha wanted the ice cream van turned into a helicopter; it will all make sense soon, don't you worry. It was now time for the wings to be welded on, The Fuzz Cats helped with this. I watched Betty put all her welding gear on, now, most welders usually wear dirty old black overalls right, but of course Betty's ultra clean overalls were bright pink. Penelope Jones was very excited about all this, she belly-danced under the splashy sparks like Shakira, while Betty welded away. Being a ghost, Penelope could get as close as she wanted; all the splashy hot sparks showered right through her, most things went through

Penelope Jones, but she could touch stuff if she wanted to. The old wrinkly boxer-girl suddenly spoke up, "Oh I say, this is just the kind of treat I've been hoping for, a nice sizzling sparkling hot shower, how delicious, all I need now is some spicy hot volcanic lava syrup for shampoo." Penelope's kooky nature made me smile. Attaching the wonky wings to the van was quite a task, the electric strength of The Fuzz Cats made things much easier, they firmly held the wings in position, while sweaty Betty welded the morning away. This super trooper Tom-boy legend didn't stop working till the job was done. Once the wings were on, Betty went straight to work on creating a helicopter engine. Sasha wanted the old Titanic propeller to be the helicopter blades sitting on top; it was a pretty cool idea. I'll get back to the helicopter project soon. Taking a break from watching the welding crew sweat it out, I decided to go back down into the secret hideout cave. I found Sasha and Kelly snooping around down there, with excited eyes, Kelly studied Betty's turbo-powered-nitro-rocket-roller-skates – they looked fun and dangerous, she obviously wanted to give them a test-run. I was quite interested in having a go on Betty's dinosaur 'T-Rex fang' skateboard. I wanted to find a big hill and let it rip, but there was no time for outings like that, we were on a tight schedule, every second had to be used wisely. Sasha spent his minutes sorting through Betty's jet-powered-rocket-ironing-board collection – he was looking for a good fast one.

"Hey Sasha," I said. "I reckon Meg must be getting close to releasing all those awful mini witches by now. What do you think, Boss?"

"Yes, not long now, honey." he said. "We need to be absolutely ready - that's all that matters, my love." I agreed, as I slipped Betty's skateboard under my arm and went back up to the street. I wasn't stealing it; I swear, I just wanted to borrow it for a while, he-he. Back up on the street, Betty was halfway towards creating a magnificent helicopter engine. A big bulk of the work had already been done, let me explain. Betty had recently been working hard on creating a brand new fantastic deluxe washing machine, one that spun at crazy speeds. She wanted to make a super fast spinner that washed, dried and ironed clothes in four minutes flat. That was her original ambitious idea, but now her fantastic deluxe dynamite turbo washer had a new destiny. Using her power-tools and talents, she converted the wild washer into a high-speed-perfect-performance-helicopter-engine, sounds like a complex operation to me, but it was child's-play for Betty's brain. After one hour of tinkering she got The Fuzz Cats to fetch the Titanic propeller. Everything was slowly coming together. Pure teamwork strikes again, in a smooth stylish groovy harmonious fashion. Betty was a tenacious mechanic, she worked relentlessly, like a little ant. I must be honest here, I was getting pretty excited about this project, more than I thought I would. Well, let me tell you something, that big old Titanic propeller turned out to be the cherry on top. Betty's SUPERSONIC HELICOPTER ICE CREAM VAN was completely futuristic! A proper chopper, I tell thee. It looked good enough to be on the front cover of a book. She put everything together like a genius, and she really appreciated the help she got from The Fuzz Cats; they made all the back-breaking donkey-work look easy. Betty bolted everything down, making sure the van was safe and flight-worthy. The new engine looked bold and beefy. Advanced mechanics is without a doubt Betty's area of expertise; 'Avant-Garde-Machinery' is her forte. It's all above me, I Avant-Garde-a-clue-myself. Ha! Betty wanted to give the ice cream van's normal engine a quick service. The Fuzz Cats agreed. A check up was long overdue, we got busy changing the oil, replacing the filters, fitting new spark plugs, Betty changed the slippery fan belt, and after giving it a sweet little tune-up, it ran like a dream. After that, we checked over the helicopter engine just one last time. Everything was set and ready to go, so Betty started her up. Well slap me sideways, the engine sang like a choir of wild rugged angels, it sounded like a keen machine ready to make its maiden voyage up to the skyways. The sweet 'hiss' of the spinning Titanic propeller grew louder as it picked up more speed. It soon created a windy storm or swirling pandemonium, old newspapers and loose litter blew all over the streets. This unique-futuristic helicopter-aircraft-sound soon caught the attention of Sasha and Kelly, they popped-up from under the street to check out Betty's magnificent work. The sun was coming up now, but it was still too early to have such a loud engine running, it sounded like a dragster car with a turbo jet. Swiftly swiping his right hand under his chin, Sasha instructed Betty to 'cut the engines.' When the Titanic propeller finally came to a halt, we suddenly heard a new distant hissing sound. At first we thought something was up with the new engine, maybe there was a tiny hole in one of the air valves? Ding! Guess again guys. The hissing sound persisted, and it suddenly became too loud to be described as background noise, it gave out a chronic creepy type of feeling, to me it sounded like a buzzing swarm of killer bees, out on the prowl. After thirty more seconds we all wised-up to what was going on, the 'hiss' was a multitude of crazy giggles coming from the bellies of wild-ruthless-yukky-disgusting-puke-face witches.

"Is that what I think it is?" Asked Fuzz Cat Sam.

"I think so," replied Sasha. The witch army were coming straight for us. Penelope Jones spoke up, "Sweet Jumpin' Jalapeno peppers, this is it! This is absolutely fantastic!"

We all looked at her in disbelief. She smiled and said,

"I mean, it's terrible. It's awful – let's make a run for it."

She looked at us with puppy eyes, then she shrugged her shoulders. Penelope was ready to fight, I think she was getting a dose of her old 'boxers adrenaline rush.' Wild feelings of pure-combat-fighting-energy took over her bones, back in her illegal boxing days, she called this her… 'Getting-psyched-up-to-fight-mode,' it was a ritual for her. No doubt this was all triggered-off by the growing danger around us. We had a brand new mission now, our next goal was simple, we had to… STAY ALIVE, AND GET THE HELL OUT OF DODGE CITY! I suddenly noticed that Kelly Ann was now wearing Betty's nitro-powered-rocket-roller-skates, she wanted to give them a good run for their money, and I was more than happy to try out Betty's dinosaur-fang skateboard. It was turning out to be a crazy morning in London Town, thousands of witches were arriving now, yikes! Waves of fear consumed my whole body, but I quickly decided not to be intimidated by these green gruesome gits. My rib began to counter-act all my feelings, turning my fear into excitement, my confidence was growing, oh yes! The time had come for us to step into the next stage of Sasha's highly organised masterplan, we needed to duck and dive our way over to Camden Town, as quickly as possible. It was time to ride with pride through the busy streets of London, come on guys, let's go!

CHAPTER 19
IT'S ALL GOING DOWN, IN CAMDEN TOWN

Well kiss my grits, I was blown away by the number of rat-ugly-witch-freaks floating up there in the blue morning sky. Thousands of green-snotty-nosed-slag-bags all staring down at us, what a bunch of losers. Roaring Meg had finally set them free, and these witches were loco-livid! Sweet lord, we were in big trouble. They badly wanted to get their revenge on Sasha. They knew he was the one responsible for trapping them inside that marble prison, all those years ago. Roaring Meg ordered all the witches to go straight to Betty's laundromat, and get rid of the whole gang by whatever means necessary, what a delightful old pig she is. Meg was pretty messed up, she stayed up on the moon, knocking back several more bottles of whiskey I reckon, she had her army to do her dirty work now. These mini witches flew all over the place, their eyes were filled with blind rage. I'll never forget their faces, they looked angry, but they also looked old, jaded and knackered. I remember fearing them, but I also remember feeling pity for them. They looked like crusty old zombies coming out of the graveyard, searching for the will to have one more pop at trying to take over the world, they looked way past their prime; it was all quite dysfunctional really, they were thousands of years old, but they were still evil. Oh dear.

The Fuzz Cats quickly jumped back inside their ice cream van, "Stick to the plan!" Shouted Sasha. Fuzz Cat George popped his head out the window and yelled,

"Aye-aye, Captain." Fuzzy George used Portobello Road for a runway. The ice cream van sped off down the street and quickly flew up into the sky like a giant eagle. It was a funny sight to see. The Titanic propeller and beefy helicopter engine worked in perfect harmony, and the spitfire wings looked spectacular.

"Stick to the masterplan, Kelly Ann!" Shouted Sasha.

"Okey-dokey, Daddio, see you in Camden Town,"

Sasha wanted the whole gang to get over to Camden as soon as possible, this was the perfect location for the next stage of the masterplan to be executed. Sonic Sasha was ALWAYS one step ahead of the herd, praise the lord. Riding fast on Betty's cool skateboard, I stayed close to Kelly's side, while she rolled and swished down the street. The pressure was on us now.

Betty and Sasha were about to fly off on a couple of jet-powered rocket ironing boards. Sasha found a good fast one down below, but Betty's was way faster.

"Oh, hang on a minute," said Betty. "I need to quickly water my dragon-fire daffodil. I'll be back in a jiffy." Jumping off her board, Betty quickly ran into the laundromat, watered her flower, flipped the 'OPEN' sign around, and left the door ajar, for any morning customers.

"Oh for heavens sake, Betty. Hurry up girl!" Sasha didn't want to be a sitting duck, he was ready to ramble on. Betty moved so fast, she was back outside in no time, she hopped up on her board, flew over to where her dad was waiting, and SCHOOOOOOOM! They zooooomed off. Penelope Jones hovered above Kelly and I, like a brave rugged kamikaze bomber, she dashed right out in front of us, and went searching for battle, she had the spirit of a wild viking. She wanted to take the fight to the witches, well, she didn't need to look too hard, they were everywhere, flying all over the place! "Here they come!" Shouted Kelly. I looked up to the sky and felt horrified. There were thousands of witches staring down at us now, a huge green cloud of witchy weirdos blocking out the morning sun. They started to make their attack. "Quick, follow me!" Kelly Ann roller-skated at top speed, I did my best to keep up. I was very impressed with Penelope Jones. She distracted thousands of witches; they all chased her instead of us, the old girl took them off in a completely different direction, nice one Penelope. This gave Kelly and myself a quick chance to make our escape. It was a strange time to start singing, but that's exactly what Kelly did, at the top of her voice she shouted a song called, 'Fortunate Son' by Creedence Clearwater Revival. I swear, Sasha and his two girls are a family of first class danger freaks, they had a fat measure of rock n roll substance dancing in their hearts and bones. Turns out Kelly's just another wacky thrill-seeker, an out and out adrenalin junkie, just like her big sis, Betty-Boo-Boo. Speaking of the Dad-Daughter dynamic duo, Betty and Sasha shot down the street like a pair of raging runaway hot-rods, they flew into Ladbroke Grove tube station, and quickly disappeared-off into one of the dark underground train tunnels, a dangerous choice of route I thought, not so easy for the witches to follow, they'd get to Camden soon enough. I was skateboarding as fast as I could go now, or was I? Kelly suddenly reached out to grab my hand, I nearly fell off, but after a few seconds, I managed to retain my balance, she crouched down low to activate the nitro-rockets in her roller skates. Holy Shamba-Reena, as soon as she hit that button, we took off like a Ducati motorbike. We slashed through the busy streets of London like a blazing hot fire-ball! This was crazy big fun! I still have no idea how I stayed on that skateboard – it must have been the purple magic in my rib, looking after me. We made it to the top of Portobello Road in ten seconds flat, then we killed-it along Bayswater Road, overtaking taxis, buses and cars, all the way up to Marble Arch, where we continued rolling boldly-on towards Camden Town, cutting through the traffic, weaving in-and-out of all the people walking along the busy streets of London, but the flying witches were close behind, they stuck to us like bubblegum, on an old man's boot. It was a busy morning in Camden Town, there were people shopping everywhere, then the witches started turning up. Kelly decided to quickly pop-in to her Dutch barge, to grab her saxophone. She was in and out like a flash, her fast movements made the barge rock about on the still waters of the canal, she quickly played her cool sax with all her might. The sound of the saxophone was like a police siren, warning people to get out of our way, I held on to the back of Kelly's coat, while she skated through the crowded streets of Camden Town, we had a witch right on our tail now. The Fuzz Cats had also arrived in Camden, they landed over yonder, outside the Roundhouse. Driving down the main drag, they turned many heads with their cool-looking ice cream van, they were getting ready to follow the next step of Sasha's supremo-magnifico-masterplan. The morning suddenly turned dark. I looked skyward to see what was going on, it was already half-filled with a multitude of green ugly mama's. Sweet-Mama-Mia-Let-Me-Go! We now had two feisty witches behind us, they followed us down a thin foot path that ran alongside the canal. They tried to grab Kelly but missed, then the coolest thing happened! One of The Fuzz Cats jumped out from behind a brick wall and grabbed the two witches with effortless ease – it was Fuzz Cat Brian I think, the tall skinny one with big hands. Fuzzy Brian now had both these witches trapped under his arms in a double headlock, we decided to stop, look back, and watch his next move. The witches wiggled about like freshly caught marlins. Brian quickly performed a strange stunt that I'd never seen before, he gave both these witches a huge electric squeeze, a thing called a HUG-ZAP. Brian's electrostatic strength was pretty fantastic, while hugging these skinny old weasels, thousands upon thousands of fat electric sparks came blasting out of his ears, he lit up like a Catherine wheel. This 'Fuzz Cat formula' successfully electrocuted the two witches into a forty-eight hour coma, a 'two-day' vacation from life. "See ya later," that was all Brian said, as the two witches fell flat on their faces. Kelly and I watched this crazy act with vivid inquisitiveness; it was a groovy thing to witness. Brian sparkled away like some kind of explosive star, about ready to blow, it was a very strange sight to see. I could only watch for ten seconds, the brightness was too much. After knocking the witches out cold, Fuzz Cat Bruce came along to give a helping hand. Both these cool cats quickly took the sleeping witches over to the ice cream van, they laid them down in the back with TLC. This Hug-Zap approach was Sasha's idea - we all had to honour Sasha's request about using no violence. That wasn't going to be easy, I suddenly thought about the pain I felt when my rib got taken away, this made me get crazy angry in a single heartbeat. Giving any screwy witch a good punch on the nose would have been very satisfying, no doubt about it. Oh well, I guess Sasha knew best. That whole day in Camden Town turned out to be an electric-master-blaster. The Fuzz Cats dished out thousands of hug-zaps; they had the whole area secured. They spent maybe six hours catching and hug-zapping over seven thousand witches, maybe more, the volume of sleeping witches piled-up fast. Not one single witch got killed, we just put them all to sleep instead, this was all part of the huge plan of course. Kelly Ann's saxophone tones drew many witches in, they also caught the attention of her old age pensioner friends - the wrinkly ones who like to race through the streets at night on their electric-powered motor scooters. They'd all just had their hearing-aids serviced, which meant they were able to pick up Kelly's distinct saxophone playing loud and clear. They lived in a retirement home about fifty yards away from Camden Lock, and just five minutes later, twenty of these brittle-boned racers showed up on their scooters, they happily helped Kelly and the cats trap more witches. Every single one of these old age scooter pensioners came from the city of Hull, they were a tough northern clan who called themselves the 'Hull's Angels.' All day long they trapped hundreds of witches with their unique kung-fu knitting skills. Kelly had taught them well. Nice one guys. Old people can be saggy and forgetful, and some may smell a bit funny, but they're still pretty cool. Many times on that electric 'sha-zam' day in Camden, The Fuzz Cats hug-zapped a witch who'd been completely tied up with knitting wool. This was, of course, the skilful work of The Hull's Angels. We had a serious storage problem now. What can one do when they're stuck by Camden Canal, with thousands of sleeping witches at their feet? The ice cream van was jam-packed, we stuffed hundreds of witches into Kelly Ann's Dutch barge; that was my job. It was full up now, they were dangling out the doors and popping out the portholes. I must be honest here - I really didn't like handling these wrinkly old tarts, they gave me the heebie-jeebies, they were light and crusty, fragile and stinky, and if I squeezed one too hard, I heard her bones crunch. They made me feel very uncomfortable. Sasha and Betty were very busy up in the skies above - I'll tell you more about them in a minute. Generally speaking, it was a very mad and hectic day, thousands of witches chased Kelly, Betty, Sasha, and Penelope all over the place, and every thirty seconds or so, The Fuzz Cats dumped another sleeping witch at my feet, I was beginning to go a little bit cuckoo to be honest. We had nowhere to put these tatty old runts. Oh well, there were bigger problems on the menu I guess, like the number of witches floating about up there in the sky, more and more witch-troops kept arriving at the scene. Sweet lord above please help us, this whole scenario was getting way too flip-flop-crazy-bananas for me. The Hull's Angels made excellent woolly booby traps, they looked like giant spider webs, and they worked like a charm. The whole gang had an excellent team strategy: Kelly Ann slyly drew the witches into the webs, and once they got tangled up, five or six of The Hull's Angels grabbed a witch and tied them up good, kung-fu style, and soon after that, one of The Fuzz Cats swung by to hug-zap the living daylights out of them. It was like catching big ugly dragonflies, once again, true teamwork in action.

After every single hug-zap, the buzzing Fuzz Cat always said, "See ya later, Pendejo!" I think that's Spanish.

Penelope Jones helped out a great deal too. She called my name out while hovering high above Camden Lock, the crazy old ghost had something she wanted to show me.

"Hey Louise, check this out, I've just invented a brand new sport. It's called SKY-BOXING." She ducked-low inside a weeping willow tree, and waited for the next ugly-snot-face-witch to zoom by, two seconds later, Penelope jumped out and gave the unlucky passing witch a swooping left power-punch upper-cut, this was immediately followed by a thunderous lightning right-hook. This double whammy punch combination knocked the witch out cold. This was Penelope's mighty Mike Tyson manoeuvre. The witch fell to the ground and soon got hug-zapped by Fuzz Cat George, or was it Fuzz Cat Sam? I can't remember to be honest. Some cool fuzzy dude for sure. Penelope sure loves her boxing, she did this dirty work behind

Sasha's back, she's a cheeky old girl. Lots of witches flew after her that day, but she kept escaping by flying through solid brick walls, the witches didn't realise she was a ghost, they followed and crashed every time. They'd be on the floor in a dizzy daze, and after five or ten seconds, another Fuzz Cat came along to hug-zap their old bones away. "See ya later, bambina!" The Fuzz Cats were having a field day. They constantly dropped witches at my feet like faithful gun dogs, and I still didn't have a clue where to put these suckers. I piled them up along-side the canal. I'll tell you more about that in a minute. Sasha and Betty were just about coping in their perimeter; they had two forms of defence. Betty had a huge bag of exploding bangers and meatballs, and Sasha had a big pocket filled with flying saucer sweets, they weren't normal flying saucer sweets, they contained a powder filled with large amounts of fresh garlic mixed with purple magic. Every time a witch got close, Sasha quickly put a flying saucer in his mouth, huffed a magic puff of wind, and a stinky mass of magic garlic breath knocked the witch out cold. They soon fell to the ground and got zing-fired by the nearest Fuzz Cat. I think being trapped in that marble prison for all those years made these stinky witches rusty flyers; some needed 'L' plates, they flew like blind old ladies with road rage, dopey demented divas with a death-wish. They were easily over ten thousand years old; they probably needed glasses, some of them had no eyes at all, they flew like bats. The exploding bangers and meatballs worked exceptionally well. Betty used these magical meat snacks like a magician. They blew-up in the witches face, turned to dust, and quickly put several witches under a sleepy spell in mid-air, they'd slowly drift down to the ground like snowflakes, and soon after, they got flash-panned by another Fuzz-Cat-Hug-Zap. It was a most extraordinary day in Camden Town. A wild electric riot! By the end of the afternoon, I was completely exhausted and overwhelmed. We now had a humongous pile of sleeping witches stacked up high, right beside Kelly's Dutch barge, the witch-pile followed the footpath up and over the steel canal bridge, there were witches everywhere! Looking over yonder, to the far side of the canal, I suddenly saw a huge construction site standing in the not-so-far-away distance. Hello Ducky, it looked like a brand-new block of apartments were going up, but it was no way finished. I guess it was about halfway done, the building stood naked, looking like a huge stack of concrete shelves. I quickly got Sasha's attention and suggested that we use this empty new building to store all the surplus witches, just for the next twelve hours or so. Sasha took one quick look at the naked building and smiled, he cheered and laughed as he spoke out loud, "Yep, that's the ticket Louise. Well spotted, honey bun."

We kept busy for the next half hour transporting all the sleeping witches over to the brand-new building. The Fuzz Cats did most of the lifting and shifting; the concrete shelves got filled-up in no time. Then I looked up to the sky again. Ah man! More sodding witches kept turning up. I wish they were all butterflies instead, that would have been a sweet dream. I tried my best to stay optimistic, I guess it was the purple magic in my system enabling me to keep a positive-mental-outlook. This whole day felt like a mad crazy dream, it just kept going on and on, hour after hour. We WERE making progress, but it was difficult to see. We WERE thinning the numbers down, I guess we just had to persevere - keep on keeping on - as the wise men say. Straight out of the blue, Sasha suddenly shouted over to me. He was desperate to get my attention.

"Hey Louise!" he said.

"Yes-Sir-Sasha-Sir-Boss-Sir!" I cheerfully shouted. I was standing on the roof of Kelly's Dutch barge, still passing witches down to The Fuzz Cats. To help speed things up, I started passing two at a time, but their heads kept falling off, so I went back to just one at a time. I guess I needed to handle them with more care. I quickly looked over to Sasha, to see what he wanted, he looked about-ready to throw something at me. "Check this out my little angel, make sure you catch this sweet little gem." Laughing his head off, Sasha threw something that looked like a pound coin, or maybe it was an acorn? I wasn't sure to be honest, but when I caught it, I quickly discovered that it was nothing more than a tiny piece of pure potent purple magic, and just before I caught it, I heard Sasha say …

"Get ready for another heart visit, Lou-Bee-Lou. Ha-ha! See ya later alligator!"

What!? Oh, Noooo!

I spontaneously disappeared from Camden Town, and suddenly found myself heading straight over to New Zealand. Holy Wagon Wheels!

I got ZIP-SLASHED over to Max Redwood and The Paradox Twins in just a few seconds, it all happened at the speed of light. ZING!! POW!! TING! BAD-A-BING-BONG!! The magic took me over to the other side of the world in three point six seconds.

Not too shabby at all.

I was suddenly back inside Max Redwood's little heart.

Holy MUNKA-TUNKA!

Here we go again.

Deep down inside, I was feeling pretty glad about this y'know.

I was yearning for a change of scenery. Maybe Sasha picked this up, yes, he probably felt my desire for change deep inside his unique purple rib, the one inside my body.

Cheers Mr Sonic x

CHAPTER 20

A QUICK PIT-STOP AT JENNIE'S

Sasha wanted me to check-up on Max and the Twins, see what they were up to. Well I must tell ya, looking out onto the world through the eyes of Max Redwood was quite something, it was like being inside my own little private cock-pit, we flew so high above the ocean, it was an awesome feeling. I was more than happy to be away from all those grotesque, vomit-head witches, urrggh, they were nothin but a rancid bunch of freaky-puke-pots. Good old Max soared right at the top of the sky, about eleven miles over the South Pacific Ocean. I saw New Zealand way over yonder. I thought The Twins would've had this 'pick-up' done and dusted by now. Oh well, New Zealand is pretty far away I guess, it's not like they were popping over to Brixton to pick up a new exhaust pipe for the spinner. Things made more sense when Max told me about their unscheduled visit to Cuba. Leon wanted to swing by Havana, to buy a few boxes of fresh Cuban cigars, typical hey. As I looked down, I saw half a dozen witches chasing the twins. Ah man! More green batty zipper-heads. Four of them were chasing Leon's flying triumph motorbike, while the other two chased after Tigerlips in the spinner. We were flying over the South Island now, looking straight ahead I suddenly saw the little white lighthouse, it stood all alone on a flat beach. Max quickly began his decent, the (not so big) lighthouse stood right at the tip of the shore, it was an old white one, and it flashed a purple light.

"That's got to be Tuhawaiki Point," I said.

"Right you are, Louise, right you are," whistled Max. Excellent, this heart visit was so much easier than the last one - more space inside Max's little heart, and this time there was no heavy lifting involved, what a sweet result.

Gazing down at the lighthouse, I saw an old woman roll out the front door, she was in a wheelchair, and she was holding something that looked like a magic wand. Like a teachers's pet she shot her hand right up to the sky and quickly threw out a huge thunderous lightning spell, and all six witches fell to the ground in seconds, like autumn leaves they drifted down towards the beach and remained motionless. Leon immediately followed them down, landing his IRON JOHN motorbike gracefully on the sand. It was a nice spacious beach, wide and flat, a popular spot for surfers. After landing with smooth perfection, Leon slowly pulled-up next to the lighthouse, switched his engine off, slid his biker goggles up over his bumpy spam, lit a cigar, and began to watch 'Evel Knievel's Best Jumps' on youtube, on his iphone. Max and I were hovering just above him. Tiger approached the lighthouse next, he cruised through the choppy waves at top speed, and he pushed the 'turbo-wash' button just at the right time, perfect timing was absolutely crucial with this, thankfully Tiger was a natural, the spinner switched back into a fancy race car just as it crossed over from sea to land. It was a pretty cool transformation to watch. Max suddenly decided to land on Leon's shoulder – a gutsy move I thought. Looking over at the lighthouse, I suddenly became quite intrigued by this mysterious lighthouse lady. 'Jennie' looked pale and jaded, but there was a wisdom in her eyes. It's hard to explain, I guess what I'm trying to say is, she looked like the kind of woman who'd lived an interesting, extraordinary life, she struck me as a deep soul, a caring loving female. As we got closer, I saw that she had no legs at all, instead she had a big flappy fin. Great Scott! Hey! This old bird was a mermaid, a very old one, maybe a pensioner. Her fin looked brilliant, lots of green shiny scales sparkling and gleaming like glitter in the sun. "Howdy, we've come on behalf of Sonic Sasha," said Tiger, blimey, he got here fast, he bowed his head to show some respect for the way Jennie took care of the six witches. "We're here to collect Sasha's supply of purple magic," Jennie was slow to answer, she looked rigid, stubborn, and very upset. She'd been Sasha's lover for a long time; and I think she still loved him. Max told me that Sasha and Jennie were old flames, they loved each other passionately…maybe a bit too much …kind of like Richard Burton and Elizabeth Taylor. Too many highs and lows.

Sasha and Jennie were together for thirty five years! Holy-Moly-Angelina-Jolie, that's a long time! Max told me that Jennie is the mother of Betty and Kelly Ann. Max was a gossiping little gremlins, he told me all the juicy facts, he explained how Jennie and Sasha had a very deep connection, but they always fought, they clashed right from the get-go, they tried to be healthy parents, but things were so difficult for them – they were under a lot of stress. I guess it's hard for a wizard and a mermaid to find some kind of mutual ground for harmonious compatibility. It's not like they were a couple of hobbits working the land together, growing pumpkins. Opposites attract I guess, but sometimes things just aren't meant to be, it must have broken Jennie's heart when they split-up, letting go and having to move on, when you're still in love, really sucks, apparently. This seemed to be the case with Jennie. Taking a good long look at the old girl, I suddenly noticed that her one-of-a-kind wheelchair was pretty unique, it was a big fish tank on wheels. The bottom half of Jennie's body had to stay underwater, all the time. It was absolutely vital that she kept her fin wet, twenty-four-seven. Jennie finally spoke up. "Sasha's purple magic." She said, with a rude unapologetic tone in her voice. "I'm glad you guys have finally come to collect it. I'm sick of doing favours for that Wishy-Washy-Weirdo." Jennie looked exhausted, but her eyes glistened with joy when Sasha's name was mentioned, the nasty things she said didn't ring true, she still had strong undeniable feelings for Sasha, emotions came up from within, and filled her eyes with love, the eyes never lie my friend. She went on,

"I've been looking after his flipping purple magic for far too long." Jennie swivelled her fish-tank-wheel-chair around with snappy impatience, she left black smudgy tire marks everywhere, she rolled back into the lighthouse and reached down for an old brown leather suitcase that was strategically tucked away, just behind the front door. This battered old suitcase was jam-packed full of purple magic. Jennie slowly dragged it out, and like a fed-up airport baggage handler, she grumpily threw it down on the old worn-out wooden porch panels. She must have known we were coming. "Here it is, take it with pleasure!" She said.

Poor Jennie, she looked so unhappy. The case popped open when it hit the old wood-decking, and there it was… All Sasha's purple magic, sitting inside, looking like a massive bar of purple transparent soap; it glowed with a cool mellow light, it was a kind of electric-lilac-moon-colour, it had a beautiful warm vibe oozing out from it.

"That's all of it." Jennie's grumpy voice sighed with an air of relief. This meant closure for her, at last, she could say bon voyage to all those lingering emotions that stuck to her heart like faded unwanted tattoos. She was glad to see it go, she had that old brown suitcase stashed away in her lighthouse for years. Leon flicked out his kickstand and slowly walked over to Jennie, like an old stubborn cowboy. We flew off his shoulder and quickly landed on Tiger's head, but he shock us off immediately, so we flew up to the top of the lighthouse, to have a look inside, nothing too exciting up there, just a humungous bulb sitting all alone, behind a thick pane of glass, we zoomed back down and landed on Tiger's shoulder, he was alright with that. Leon paused as he knelt down in front of the open suitcase, he was taking it all in, he looked like a Russian hit-man inspecting his weapon, his stone-cold-blue 'Paul Newman' eyes looked so cool. Never in a hurry, he closed the case, picked it up, stood up straight and looked the old spinster mermaid right in the eyes. Jennie was completely unafraid to look back at Leon's weird 'tree-bark' face, they both stared at each other in silence for ten minutes, the intensity of this was beautiful. "I say, you're a funny-looking fellow, aren't you? I think a nice weekend break at Disneyland Paris would be a good move for you, boy." Jennie suddenly burst out laughing, and so did Tiger. Leon wasn't very good with manners, he didn't smile or laugh at all. The old wolf couldn't give a damn about petty jokes. He just stared at Jennie for ten more seconds, took a big lug on his cigar, blew the smoke out and slowly walked back to his motorbike, nothing seemed to bother this old beast. The laughter bounced off him like wedding confetti. Leon carefully tucked the old leather suitcase inside IRON JOHN'S sidecar, he made sure it was strapped in good and proper. Tiger suddenly jumped high over the spinner and ran across the flat beach, he went to collect the six unconscious witches sleeping on the sand. Hovering just above, Max and I watched him toss the witches over his shoulders, he threw them around his neck like long flimsy seaweed scarves, walking back to the spinner he looked like a cowboy wearing a big green ugly poncho, he quickly dumped the witches in the back, on the old red chesterfield sofa, that sofa was ripped-up pretty bad, it had spillage splats all over the seats, a mixture of sea-spray, strawberry-jam-donut-stains, and dried up coffee puddles, a nice present left by the chubby couple back in West London. That ragged old sofa needed a good wipe down. Tiger's ultra sharp nose picked up the sweet scent of all the sugary jam smudges, so before squashing all the witches into position, he got busy licking all the coffee and jam off the faded covers, what a crazy old cat. He probably got a good taste of the salty seawater too. After licking the sofa, he licked his paws, then he sat all the witches in a line with their hands by their sides, it was a snug fit. They sat side by side on that sofa, all with their heads bowed down, they looked totally wasted, Jennie must have thunder-bolted them with a fierce stun-gun spell, something similar to the mighty bold Fuzz-Cat-Hug-Zap. They were long gone. Max and I both agreed that we wanted to feel the energy of the purple magic, so we flew over and landed on the handlebars of Leon's motorbike, but the wolf-man was still busy puffing on his cigar, and Max doesn't like cigar smoke, neither do I to be honest, they flippin stink, so we decided to swish over to Jennie instead, it was important to be polite and say hello. Max landed on her bony old shoulder. "Oh, my lord, is that you, Max?" Jennie's voice suddenly perked up, she was more cheerful and light-hearted now. Max tapped into a deeper love inside her. "Hello, my old friend." Max and Jennie were good pals back in the day. She turned her head to whisper something into the robin's little ear. I heard every word, of course. "Tell Sasha I will always love him, and please tell him that I can always be found deep in the ocean. If he needs me, I will happily return." This mystical-mermaid-woman still had a universe of love in her heart, and it was all for Sonic Sasha. I guess it's hard to just switch love off, if it's true and authentic, it never really dies, well that's what I've heard anyway. This seemed to be the case with Jennie the mermaid lady. She was awfully pleased to see Max, but deep down inside, she was so tired, and uninspired. She looked unloved, and this made my heart sad. She gently coaxed Max off her shoulder and held him up in her hand. Not wasting one second, Max perched himself up on her wrinkly old index finger. Jennie finally smiled, yeah baby. She gave Max a little kiss on the side of his head,

"I'll be on my way now, Mr Redwood," she whispered.

"I am no longer needed here, at last, I can go back home, back to the ocean, back to where I truly belong."

With a vague smile Jennie suddenly took her magic wand out, and proceeded to sprinkle a glittery spell all over herself, tiny pieces of shiny stardust poured out from the wand, like sparkling water falling from a large shower head, the sparks glowed extra-bright-white, like miniature electric snowflakes. Jennie delivered this spell with professional perfection, and when the spell was cast, she tossed the wand over to Tigerlips, he caught it with ease.

"Give this wand to Kelly Ann, Tiger-man," she said. We felt a sudden shift of energy in the air, the wind changed its mind and suddenly blew in the opposite direction. Max felt this and quickly decided to fly back over to Leon, this time we stood on the headlamp of IRON JOHN. Jennie suddenly started to levitate, she was floating high above her wheelchair now. Hello, what's this all about? Seawater dripped from her beautiful mermaid fin, she climbed ten meters high, and after sixty drippy seconds she started spinning around and around, this precious old lady was gradually turning into a colourful twisting gust of wind. This was spectacularly awesome, and very unexpected. We watched Jennie spin gracefully through the sky, she was slowly hovering back towards the ocean, it was a beautiful vision to observe. We gazed-on with wonder as she gently flew further and further out into the mystic, then suddenly, she turned back into a young beautiful mermaid. What?! She splashed into the sea like a happy dolphin, and that was it, she was gone, but wait, after five more seconds her fin popped up to wiggle a quick wave. I guess that was her way of saying goodbye. Sweet Jamaica, that was pretty to watch. She swam off into another world, free at last, bless her soul. Tiger spoke up. "Well, there's something you don't see every day." He examined the magic wand and immediately started using it as a toothpick, he kept busy removing dried-up bits of sticky-old-strawberry-jam-blobs from his sharp teeth, then he safely tucked the wand away, stashing it inside his leather jacket. Max suddenly moved very fast now, without any warning he jumped up from the headlamp and started to flap and hover directly in front of Leon's face. The cheeky robin purposely used the tips of his wings to flick all the hot ashes away from Leon's cigar, he did this for several seconds, till the cigar was completely extinguished. Leon was not impressed. Faster than Jackie Chan he caught Max in mid-air, and for the longest moment he squeezed and stared the little robin down. "DON'T YOU EVER DO THAT AGAIN!" Leon's scratchy old sandpaper voice sounded like a cool singer called Tom Waits. Tom sings a great song called, 'Take Me Home.' Max gulped, then he whistled out a short bossy tune, and Leon released him from his grip. Leon was a scary old road warrior, but I kind of liked his dangerous energy. Straight after that, both The Paradox Twins started their engines, and got ready for the next long journey, it was time for all of us to head back to England. Old Blighty here we come.

The next part of the plan was to catch up with the rest of the gang, back in London. A rendezvous at Highgate Cemetery had been arranged. Now, to avoid being seen by any more disgusting witches, we decided to fly under the world, instead of around it. It was safer and quicker to fly directly over the South Pole, then shoot up past Africa, dash over Spain and France, glide over Brighton and head straight for London. Leon flew high above, while Tigerlips sped through land and sea below. Max continued flying at a much higher altitude – this was the best place to be, when you're on the look-out for witches.

Tiger sped the spinner speedboat at top speed. Bopping along the waves he passed by a place called Betty's Bay, in South Africa, this was the spot where he made a surprise unscheduled stop at a petrol garage. Tiger urgently needed some rope, he wanted to strap the six witches down, get them properly tied to the sofa, the old girls were bouncing all over the place. Tiger found a tow rope, but he didn't have any money to pay for it, so he decided to improvise with the magic wand. The old man serving behind the counter was completely bald, and had no teeth. This made Tiger take a gamble, he wanted to try and help the old fella, do something nice for him y'know. Tiger took the wand out and childishly zapped the old man right in the face, and he suddenly grew a full head of hair, and two seconds later, he developed a full set of white shiny teeth! The old guy was so happy, he jumped about while looking in the mirror, his new teeth had tiger fangs, but he didn't mind all that much. To show his appreciation, the old man happily gave Tiger a tow rope, along with some beef flavoured crisps, soft drinks, and chicken and bacon sandwiches, plus several big boxes of non-biological washing powder.

Nice one Tigerlips, what a kind crafty cat you are.

Tiger was back on the move in no time, cruising through the choppy waves, he headed straight up the west coast of Africa. This was the quickest route back to old England. Max, myself and Leon were miles ahead, flying fast and high, while Tiger played catch-up. We all hoped and prayed for a witch-free journey back to grubby old London, and that's exactly what we got.

Get in there my son!

CHAPTER 21

A RENDEZVOUS AT THE GRAVEYARD

It was kind of cool being back in Highgate, the cemetery felt really spooky y'know. I looked like 'steam leaving a kettle' when Max breathed me out into the cool night air, I slowly turned back into my usual 'weird' kooky self, ha-ha. London felt so old, you could almost taste the history in the air, I liked being back in the exact same spot where Betty saved my life, it made me feel grateful about many things, being part of this cool gang was a blessing, all these peculiar individuals felt like family to me now, they were my tribe, they *looked* dysfunctional, but all their actions were full of good intentions. To speak from the heart, I can honestly say that it was an absolute pleasure being in their company. I'll always remember those two lonely years, before I met Betty, boy O boy they really sucked! Oh well, best not to dwell on the past. We chilled under the wisdom of the tall whispering chestnut trees, perhaps they were oaks? Or London planes? I don't know, it was too dark to tell. It had been a true-blue-wacky-bing-bang-boo kind-of-day, a real busy one filled with many unorthodox activities. Nobody disturbed us in the old graveyard; we had all the privacy we needed, some ghost flew about, but they caused no bother, they just wanted to see Penelope Jones, she's a celebrity ghost y'know, she's probably more famous now than when she was alive. I walked over to help Tiger untie the six witches from the spinner sofa, we carefully laid them down in the back of the ice cream van. I was impressed by all the good news I heard, the whole gang had performed exceptionally well, and we mustn't forget the Hull's Angels, they did a great job too, no doubt they were back in their retirement home, probably all with their feet up watching 'The Fast and Furious part 7.' The whole operation in Camden Town turned out to be a fantastically-successful-mission, a highly charged 'Hug-Zappa-Rama-Day,' that will no doubt go down in history. Sonic Sasha was right when he said, 'TEAM WORK MAKES THE DREAM WORK.' I asked him…"So what's next, boss?" He replied in a cheeky cowboy voice, "Well, little lady, we gotta great deal of sleepin witches to take over to Hudson Bay, we got many pick-up-points-to-pass-by, first off we gotta collect the sleeping witches in Betty's Portobello laundromat, and after that we gotta dig out all the lazy witch girls sleepin in Kelly's Dutch barge, then we gotta fetch all the stacked-up witches sittin and waitin in the new block a flats, on the construction site, by the canal." Fuzz Cat George suddenly spoke up,

"Oh I say, I've just remembered, while stacking those witches-up high, I recall one of them falling off the ledge and landing head first into a big industrial cement mixer, I must remember to pop down there and pick her up, on our return." George had

a nice smile. I spoke up next,
"We also have six fresh witches sleeping in the back of The Fuzz Cat's ice cream van."
"Quite right, Louise, quite right, excellent work guys" Sasha patted Tiger and myself on the back, he had more witch info to blurt out, "We must also swing past Lord's cricket ground." Sasha was giggling out loud. "There's a huge pile of about three thousand witches sleeping there now, dead centre on the immaculate green cricket square." Sasha's laughter invited the rest of the gang to laugh along with him. I detected a fine slice of confident, egocentric pride circulating through everyone's mind that evening, it was understandable, we did a lot of work that day, I guess we were all quite pleased and happy with ourselves. It had been a hard day's night, or a hard night's day, something like that, I think I had a dose of jet-lag, it certainly was a great deal of hard work; that's what I'm trying to say. The good news was this... Everything was moving in the right direction, and that was all that really mattered.
"What about Roaring Meg?" I asked.
"What's she up to?" I wondered.
Sasha's eyes suddenly dimmed down, they looked all sad and heavy now,
"I think she's still up on the moon, Lou-Bee-Lou."
"She's probably watching TV, drinking the hours away, she's a wild hearted whiskey-a-go-go-girl now, oh dear."
"Well blow me down." I said. Sasha continued,

"She's gotten worse over the years, y'know, she's definitely losing her marbles."

Sasha put his hands over his face.

"Poor Meg," he said. Sasha really felt sorry for her. He wanted to save Meg from the dark will that poisoned her mind, heart, body and soul. I sometimes wonder if that's possible? It's a tall order, I guess time will tell.

It was around eight thirty in the evening, and we were all slowly beginning to unwind. Leon got a nice little fire started, and we all gathered round it. Kelly Ann curiously walked over to the Iron John motorbike, she wanted to check out the purple magic, she carefully pulled the old battered suitcase out from the rusty old side-car and proceeded to open it up for all to see, this magic had a 'fresh-wild-lavender' scent to it, a calm feeling of peace oozed-out from this purple mass of energy, it chilled everyone out in seconds, and it also made the campfire flames roar up in glory. In that fleeting moment, I saw the light of the flickering flames dance all over the faces of everyone present, such magnificent extraordinary faces. I was hanging out with the coolest, wildest 'black-sheep-outcasts' on planet earth. Max was happy to be sitting back on Sasha's shoulder, I looked over and saw how Kelly and Tiger had gotten themselves into a nice cosy laid back cuddle, they were all smooched up, chilling with their backs leant up against a big tree trunk, they were happily gazing into the fire, chatting and giggling away. Tiger took Jennie's magic wand out from his jacket pocket and gave it straight to his new girlfriend. Kelly's face lit up with excitement, then Betty put her arm around me, she was so kind and sweet, she made me feel rich and blessed; I felt like I was a genuine member of the gang now. Fuzz Cat Sam suddenly stood up and walked over to the ice cream van, to fetch his old ukulele, he quickly tuned the strings and started strumming away, he sang lots of mellow songs for us, this gentle music created a nice calming Sunday night atmosphere, but I think it was Wednesday, hey-ho. Sam's voice was very soothing, he seemed to purr and meow while he sang, it sounded sweet, delightful, groovy and strange. We all slowly slipped into a nice relaxed state of mind. Leon and Betty started puffing away, she took her pipe out while Leon shoved his face right into the fire, to light a new Cuban cigar. "You really ought to quit that nasty habit, y'know," said Sasha, he was not too pleased to see his daughter smoking. "Yes, it's stupid to smoke, why mess your lungs up? It makes no sense at all," said Penelope, being a ghost she decided to sit right in the middle of the fire, she liked showing off. Betty replied almost instantly. "Oh, I don't care what you guys say, I like smoking my pipe from time to time, I'm a cosmic feminine wonder girl, with nerves of steel. I enjoy the occasional puff on my pipe, this is how I roll baby. I'll quit one day." Sasha looked at me, then he rolled his eyes up. Leon looked like he had something to say now… he looked Betty right in the eyes and said, "Why smoke, when you're already smoking hot?" The cosy music suddenly stopped, ha-ha, this compliment took everyone by surprise, Betty didn't know what to say, she turned raspberry red. Leon boldly expressed his fiery feelings for her in one suave sweeping question. He didn't care if the whole world knew. Leon was growing on me, he was terribly cool, his dangerously intense-natural-energy was infectious, he was like a stick of dynamite, the last guy in the room you wanted to upset believe me, being close to Leon felt like being close to a volcano, he might go off any minute, it was kind of tantalising. Our attention suddenly got drawn to Fuzz Cat Bruce now, he was in a deep sleep, making lots of buzzing sizzling sounds, the silly cat was still hug-zapping witches, deep down in his dream. We all laughed as he wiggled and squirmed about on the ground, maybe he was having a wet dream, ha-ha. Tiger reached over to gently wake him up, "Wakey-Wakey, old boy, come on now, it's only a dream." Bruce jumped right out of his skin, he thought Tiger was a witch, he proceeded to give him a big-bad-buckaroo-grizzly-bear-hug-zap. It made such a loud crackling noise. Tiger's bones rattled away, while silver sparks flew everywhere, "Heeeeeeeey, stop that you crazy fruitcake, it tickles!" Tiger was trying to act cool in front of Kelly Ann, but he looked pathetic, he jolted about like a jagged raver listening to techno music, he acted like he'd just been tasered, being one-third electric eel, Tiger probably enjoyed all the extra voltage, he was smoking happy now. Bruce fully woke up. "Oh no! Sweet fudge-a-dairy, sorry about that, dude." All the hair on Tiger's head smoked and crackled like used black matches, it was extra frizzy now, we all laughed. Even Leon smiled, well, it was more of a tiny smirk really. "Ah, that's ok, no worries pal," said Tiger. "It felt quite good actually." Tiger suddenly found himself in a happy-dizzy-daze, this made Kelly want to comfort her new boyfriend, she reached out to put her arm around him, but she got the biggest shock of her life. She got fire-snapped by all the electro-static energy in Tiger's system, she flew right up into the sky, and on her way back down, she landed in a tree and woke up a sleeping owl. Ha! Everyone laughed. Soon after we all simmered down for a spell, but the silence soon got broken by Penelope Jones, she had a burning question that she was dying to ask. "I've been wondering, guys, how the heck-fire are we going to get all these sleeping witches transported over to Hudson Bay?" This was the next stage of Sasha's masterplan, take all the witches over to Canada and dump them onto the Titanic's top deck. It was quite a unique plan, I'm glad Sasha knew what he was doing, cos the rest of the gang didn't seem to have a clue. We had a slight issue now, none of us, including Sasha, knew how to get the witches over to Canada, this problem was a bit of a stinker, a tricky one to figure out, it was the only part of Sasha's masterplan that needed some creative input. Sitting up with his legs crossed, Sasha kept busy pulling long hairs out of his nostrils. This cheeky wizard looked like he was getting a little too comfortable, he smiled a shameless grin, looked around to everyone and said…

"Anyone got any ideas?" Silence took over again, we all stared into the dancing flames while everyone's imagination ticked away, we quietly brainstormed under the bright stars. "We need to get every single witch over to the Titanic, in Hudson Bay? Well, how are we going to do that?" Asked Tiger. "I have an idea." I announced. I boldly spoke my mind. "Not so long ago, Max flew over a travelling circus in Regent's Park, they were busy setting up a huge big top circus tent. Well, maybe we could borrow their tent for a while. It looked massive, definitely big enough to bag-up and carry a humongous pile of sleeping witches."

"Bingo! That should do it," said Betty.

"Yes, I think it's a great idea," said Kelly Ann.

"Yes, I like it too," said Sasha. All the gang agreed.

Yeah baby, I Rock! Louise Buttersky at your service, always happy to help. I thank you.

Although we were all such different individuals, there was one thing we all had in common that night, all of us were completely starving, we all agreed on fish and chips for dinner. A coin flipping competition decided who'd have to walk up to Highgate Village, to collect our greasy chips and battered cod. Fuzz Cat Brian and Betty lost the toss, they briskly walked up to the High Street and soon came back with a dozen portions of cod and chips, they bought saveloys and yummy chicken pies as well. Eating with our fingers and thumbs we all got stuck-in, for ten nostalgic seconds I started thinking about my Dad, the strong smell of the fish and chips mixed with vinegar took me straight back to his restaurant, back in Devon, he's such a cheeky character, I love my old man so much. My inner thoughts suddenly got interrupted by Betty's bossy voice.

"Hey, has anyone got any more ketchup? I need a few squirts for my chips." I handed a couple of sachets to her, and that's when I saw Leon's fangs grow bigger. His vampire desires were tingling away, he mumbled something in his scratchy old wolf voice.

"I don't mind ketchup on my chips, but I much prefer a couple of shots of fresh blood, mmmm, much tastier."

"Hey, cut that out!" Said Sasha. Sasha understood Leon. He knew the wolf-man had a dark side. Looking straight at me, Leon shrugged his shoulders and said.

"Hey man, nobody's perfect."

His icy blue eyes squinted a tiny sparkle, and for the first time ever, I saw a warm light shine out from them, he was a funny old beast. I guess nobody has ever told him that it's ok for him to just be exactly who he really is. It was good to see Leon finally loosening up, I guess the take-away food helped. I think, deep down, Leon was a kind soul, very deep down. Everyone became sleepy after the fish and chips feast, but nobody went to bed, we all played frisbee instead, The Fuzz Cats had a brand new 'glow in the dark' 175 gram yellow frisbee, so, we kept busy throwing that around for a while. The next part of our big plan was simple, we had to steal the big-top circus tent down in Regent's Park, and use it for our witch-collecting expidition straight after. Most of London will be fast asleep by the time we delved into these dodgy deeds. After a good long frisbee session, we all came back and sat round the fire for a little breather. "We'll get moving just after midnight, ok guys," said Sasha. We then had a little sing-song, it was nice hearing the fire pop and snap, it complimented the sound of the ukulele playing soft and gentle, The Fuzz Cats sang many tunes, Betty and Kelly joined in. Leon wouldn't, and couldn't sing to save his life, he sat back and gazed at the stars for a while, he sometimes peeked over to watch Betty sing. Tiger tried to sing but he sounded awful, The Fuzz Cats gave him a tambourine to bash, before ordering him to stop singing. Ha-ha. My favourite song they performed that night was a number called…'Don't Worry Baby,' by The Beach Boys, the two sonic sisters harmonising with the cats sounded awesome, everyone in this gang absolutely loved music. Time flew by pretty fast, it was suddenly ten minutes after midnight, and clapping his hands twice, Sasha quickly stood up and said, "Right, my spooky-trusty companions, it's time for all of us to boogaloo down to the circus." Sasha cupped his right hand behind his right ear, he silently began to listen out to the sky, we heard a cold distant wolf-cry. "Oh I say, can you hear that, Louise? I think I just heard the Ma-Hoo-Sive BIG TOP circus tent calling out to me." This was so silly, it was Penelope Jones crouching down, howling behind the ice cream van. Sasha was jumping up and down like a kid now, "Well pluck my good-luck daisy, and slap my chops like crazy, I believe she's calling out to us from over yonder, Louise, yes! She wants to help us complete our mission. YIPPEE iA! Let's get the show on the road!" Sasha had the biggest grin, his sharp eyes glistened as he spontaneously danced around the fire, I think he was Morris dancing, he winked at me, before doing the river-dance with Penelope, oh dear, two fruit loops under the moonlight, we put out the fire and got ready to cruise down to Regent's Park. It was time to nick the Grand Circus Tent. Or were we just borrowing it? Time will tell.

CHAPTER 22

THE BUSY NIGHT SHIFT

The whole gang stayed close together for this cheeky part of our mission. We just about managed to squeeze everyone inside the ice cream van, including the six sleeping witches already stuffed-in at the back, we dropped them off at Lord's Cricket Ground first. The plan was simple, we needed to quietly 'drive' through the streets of London, the helicopter engine was far too loud, we had to be wise, the ice cream vans normal engine was smooth and quiet, it had a nice hush-hush sound to it, apart from second gear, that grindy gear moaned and whined like a donkey in need of some cough mixture.

We soon arrived at Regent's Park, tip-toeing about like foxy little midnight burglars. Keeping cool and calm we stayed in pack formation and waited for our boss to dish out some soft whispery orders. Sasha spoke up,

"Right, huddle up guys, this is a sneaky 007 operation ok, we need to be as quiet as mice, so look sharp and stay on your tippy toes, alrighty. It's gonna be a long night." Nobody noticed, but Tiger was still hanging about inside the ice cream van. He was having a good linger and snoop around, probably sniffing about for some ice cream, he didn't find any, but he soon discovered a little black box with a big red switch, the crazy cat suddenly felt compelled to go ahead and turn the switch on.

"I wonder what that does?" After hitting the switch the old ice cream van suddenly blasted out huge waves of loud childish lullaby music, it came from a big speaker under the hood. Faster than a greyhound, Fuzz Cat George ran back in to turn it off.

"Ah, come on Tiger, man. Act professional, you twit!"

"Sorry George," that was all Tiger said, as he sniggered away.

Holy smoking bananas, I was absolutely blown away when I saw the size of the circus tent - it sure was the BIGGEST MAMA I EVER SAW! The mothership of all tents. I had to tilt my head right back, so my eyes could take it all in; it was the Queen bee of all tents.

"Ok, Listen up," whispered Sasha.

"We are not here to steal this tent, ok.

We're just borrowing it for a while."

"Would that be for a long while, Daddio?" Asked Kelly Ann, with a cheeky glint of sarcasm in her light tender voice, she enjoyed joking around with her father, the love between them grew fast. Then, right out of the blue, Betty started giggling, and that made Leon snigger, and that gave The Fuzz Cats permission to laugh, Tiger was already giggling. I tried so hard not to smile, but it was too late, I started to laugh with the hiccups. We ALL had the giggles now, and there was nothing we could do about it. Sasha came up with a quick solution to solve this silly issue. He quickly conjured up a huge invisible soundproof bubble, for all of us to work in, we didn't want to disturb the travelling circus people, they were sleeping just over yonder, in their gipsy caravans. Sasha conducted many spells, but the best was yet to come. The Boombastic fantastic groovy Titanic spell was ace! I will tell you more about that soon. Sasha was a tip-top wizard, maybe the coolest ever. We quietly went to work on dismantling the huge tent, taking all the giant steel pegs out of the ground - this was much easier said than done. Those babies were whacked in good! It took ages to wiggle them out. When we finally unpegged the last pin, we tried our best to fold the tent up, it drove us nuts, so we just scrunched it up real good. We quickly tied the tents ropes to the back of the ice cream van and got ready to make a sharp exit. The ice cream van had a good strong tow bar; and I must say, it came in very handy. It was time to fly. Fuzzy George started up the fantastic helicopter engine, the Titanic propeller spun like a magnificent beauty; it was such a cool invention. Betty is one skilful tom-boy genius, respect! Hopping back into the van we quickly swooped up into the sky, when the big propeller touched Sasha's sound-proof bubble, it popped and disappeared like a soap bubble at bath time. We had to fly extra high now, we didn't want the tent to bump into any buildings below. At last, we were on our way, oh yeah baby, let's get this done. This was just the beginning of our long night shift. The crazy Fuzz Cats cheekily started singing 'Nightshift' by The Commodores. It was time to collect ALL the sleeping witches; we had many stops to make, first up was Betty's laundromat. Arriving back in Portobello Road, we quickly landed in front of her shop and proceeded to open the circus tent to the best of our ability, it was time to crack on with some speedy loading, we worked overtime like unpaid pitter patter ninja angels, silently slogging away.

Holy Peter Pancakes! When I first walked into the laundromat, I was completely blown away by what I saw, there were sleepy witches snoring everywhere. Betty's shop was ram-jammed from top to bottom. All the witches were still sleeping like happy babies, thank God. Actually, they were snoring like green-ugly-goblins. It looked like the aftermath of a huge witch party, wasted witches sprawled out on the floor, lying on top of the washing machines, slouching over the big long wooden benches, chilling in the back office, snoozing under the staircase. Some were cooped-up inside the big yellow tumble dryers. Everywhere you looked there were sleeping witches, so, one by one, we took them outside and placed them in a huge pile, in the middle of the tent. A few times during this operation I stopped to have a good long look at these green-sleepy-girlies. I got right up close, I was curious, I wanted to examine their faces, well let me tell you this…

They looked absolutely terrible. Sweet lord, some of them only had one ear, some had no teeth, some had just one arm, some had no hair - they had these big bald green slappy heads. They all looked battered and beaten up. I felt sorry for these witches; none of them looked happy, or healthy. As soon as the laundrette was empty we all formed a chain-gang and got busy bringing up the remaining witches from the secret hideout cave. I was at the end of the chain, so I got to see how Max Redwood and Penelope Jones kept busy organising the tent. They turned that huge mama inside out, and this pretty much converted it into a massive giant sack. Penelope's plan was to make the tent look like a giant punch bag, she always found a way to bring the sport of boxing into the equation, from that moment on, we started calling it the 'CIRCUS SACK.' Max and Penelope did a first-class job; all the witches got nicely 'bagged-up' in very little time. "Oh, I almost forgot," whispered Betty. "I've got two dozen witches safely stored-away, just around the corner, in my private lock-up." Betty had her own private garage, a small workspace located under a bridge, in one of the old arches, beneath the busy train tracks. This was her private workshop, she built Iron John and the Spinner in there. She makes all kinds of stuff in her lock-up, ashtrays, sculptures, armchairs, coffee-tables, musical instruments, metallic lamp shades made from old smashed-up cars, basically anything she can sell down at

Portobello Market on the weekend. Sometimes she has small private gigs in there too. Kelly and Tiger volunteered to go pick up the twenty-four sleeping witches. They hopped in the ice cream van and shot off around the corner in seconds, my goodness they were gone for ages. When they finally returned they looked terribly smug and happy with themselves. My guess is they quickly threw the witches in the back and spent twenty minutes kissing and sucking face, ha! They were a sweet couple, very odd-looking, but delightfully charming. They suited each other very well, 'opposites attract' strikes again, down in thunderbolt city.

"Well, hello there," whispered Betty, as she put her arm around her glowing little sister.

"Someone looks very pleased with themselves, don't they?" Kelly's face turned strawberry red, she'd just finished a snog-a-thon. Tiger tried to look innocent, but that's a hard thing to do when you have Kelly's purple lipstick smeared all over your face. His temporary lip gloss made him look like a cheeky Marc Bolan fan. We quickly dumped the twenty four witches in the sack, along with all the others. It was now time to put this circus tent to the test. We all grabbed the thick rope that Max and Penelope had prepared, everything was tied together, we worked hard like a bunch of enthusiastic cub scouts, stage one almost done. Sasha quickly ordered The Paradox Twins to pop back into the laundromat, it was time to do a last-minute idiot check, just in case any witches had been overlooked. Leon found one, she was sleeping inside the last yellow tumble dryer, wrapped-up in a huge bundle of beach towels, he quickly brought her out and threw her into the sack, we attached the thick ropes to the tow bar, and hurried back into the van. "Ok, all clear now," whispered Fuzz Cat George. "Oh wait, hang on a minute, guys." Penelope Jones had something to say, "Would it be alright if we all stayed at the laundromat for another fifteen minutes or so, I'd love to give my panties and boxing gloves a good wash, my knickers are all stinky."

This request made everyone laugh out loud. Sasha quickly blurted out a loud firm…"No PJ! We have too much to do. We need to keep moving you silly old girl. We have a very busy night ahead of us." Penelope sighed like a bulldog.

Everyone kept their fingers crossed as the van slowly flew up into the starry skies above. The tow bar at the back was mighty strong, Betty reinforced it with some hardcore wonder-welding, it made lots of heavy creaking sounds, but it was doing the job, so far so good. Max Redwood and Penelope Jones hovered beneath us – they wanted to keep a sharp eye on the circus sack, it swung about in the wind like a huge wrecking ball, it looked pretty weird, but it worked perfectly well, so… Hallelujah baby.

Our next stop was Camden Town, it was time to pop back to Kelly's Dutch Barge, and re-visit the construction site by the canal. This was an express visit, we took care of business nice and quick down in Camden, and we didn't forget to pick up the mucky witch sleeping in the big cement mixer. We had to move fast, time was ticking away, it was close to three in the morning, and we wanted to get out of London before the rush hour. The ice cream van picked ALL the witches up with absolute ease, our plan was moving along nice and smooth, like a sweet harmony, no glitches anywhere. Betty's custom-made helicopter engine functioned like it was made by Rolls Royce, and the robust circus-sack was hanging tough, zero problems baby. The thick canvas was ultra strong. It wasn't like the witches were fat overweight junk food lovers, they were more like skinny-old, chain-smoking crusty losers, ha! I hope I don't sound too rude.

"One more stop to make, guys," said Sasha.

"Destination: Lord's Cricket Ground."

It was a tiny ten minute flight away. The ice cream van flew high above the streets of North London, we must have been a strange sight to see, we stopped many foxes in their tracks. It's not every day you see a flying ice cream van carrying a huge circus tent full of sleeping witches.

Looking down, we saw a milkman doing his early morning round, he was driving his old milk float. I guess he heard our beefy titanic propeller engine buzzing away up above, the guy looked up and suddenly freaked out, perhaps he thought we were aliens? The silly sod weaved about on the empty streets below, and skidding out of control, he suddenly crashed his old float into a lamp post. Oops-a-daisy, there was smashed glass and puddles of milk everywhere. We laughed our heads off as we gazed down at the poor fella. Sasha opened the big hatch side-door and shouted down,

"Ahoy there, I say, we're terribly sorry about that old boy!"

Betty shouted next,

"Hey Mister, don't cry over spilt milk," The milkman grumpily looked up, and after hesitating for two seconds, he gave us the finger, ha-ha! It's funny how someone else's anger can instantly give another person immediate laughter and happiness. I love that. We flew over London Zoo next. I remember looking down at the giraffes, they were looking right back at us. I went to London Zoo with my folks once, giraffes have the biggest eyeballs, I swear. They're the size of frickin cricket balls, they're awesome creatures! I guess all the other animals were still sleeping. Arriving at Lord's Cricket Ground, we gently untied the circus sack and got busy loading up more witches. We had over twelve thousand bagged-up now, and another six thousand sitting right in front of us; on the perfectly well kept cricket green. We moved like cheeky sneaky bandits. We couldn't be too rough with these old girls; it made more sense to handle them with care. Kindness pays off. They were in a deep trance, a forty-eight-hour coma, but it was still very possible to wake them up, and if just one witch woke from her slumber, she'd no doubt go straight to work on waking all the others, and that would have created a huge nightmare scenario, the last thing we wanted was another Hug-Zap-athon. Can you Imagine that? The whole gang having to go through another insane frantic Electric-Camden-Town-Shebang, one more time. No thank you. It was wiser to use a gentle approach, keep the witches sleeping, 'Nice 'N' Easy does it', just like Frank Sinatra says. Two arduous hour of lifting and shifting swished on by, and the bag was completely full, we were pretty much ready to rock n roll over to Canada now. Every single witch had been successfully crammed into the sack, which meant the time had now come for us to put good old London in our rear view mirror.

"Hudson Bay, here we come!" Said Sasha. All the gang felt quite pleased with themselves, except for Leon the lonely wolf-man, he was in a terrible stubborn mood, he made it quite clear that he didn't want to be travelling in the ice cream van anymore. He wanted to be sitting back in the driver's seat of his flying motorcycle, he liked being alone. Leon grumpily explained that he was gonna hop in a cab and head-on back up to Highgate Cemetery, to pick up 'IRON JOHN.' He boldly broke out the cricket grounds, smashing through some pretty large glass modern doors. I decided to tag along with him, we walked out on to Wellington Road. Sasha knew we'd catch up soon enough. Leon tried his best to wave down a black taxi, but they all kept zooming past him. This old wolf seemed to put fear in every man, he quickly hid behind a tree and asked me to do the honours. I stood innocently as I held my hand out, and the first black taxi instantly pulled over, yes! Leon quickly came out from behind the tree and spoke to the cockney cab driver in his weird scratchy wolf voice, "Take me and my daughter up to Highgate Cemetery. We need to get there fast." I'll never forget the look on the driver's face when he first saw Leon. He went all pale, turning white as snow, ha! Our ride in the black taxi was quite comical, I think the sight of Leon's fangs put our taxi driver under a lot of stress. With a shaky hand he lit up a cigarette and quickly smoked it down to the butt, he then proceeded to light a second cigarette with his first one, he was mumbling lots of prayers. Leon sat in the back like a solid-gangster-legend, he was completely relaxed, as he puffed away on another fresh Cuban cigar, it just hung there from his lips, he didn't move at all, he kept as still as the Abraham Lincoln statue, over in Washington D C. Leon was happy to be heading back to his bike, this maverick vampire-were-wolf loved his own private space, but I think I was growing on him, it felt like I was beginning to reach an unspoken acceptance under his s kin.

He seemed to be quite blasé about me wanting to hang out with him, I sure came in handy from time to time, I'd be happy to wave down a taxi any day for this weird wolf, he had such an intimidating presence, I loved it. He's not scared of anyone, or anything, and nobody ever gives him any grief or trouble. Sitting beside Leon was kind of like being under the wing of a dragon. There was an 'Oliver Reed' sort of danger about him, it was terribly attractive, what can I say… Girls love a wild one! But those cigars were so damn stinky. Oh well. Maybe he'll quit some day, maybe he won't. I suddenly got the urge to turn around and look out the back window, and that's when I caught a glimpse of the ice cream van, slowly taking off into the sky. The huge circus sack was bulging now, this view was so surreal, kind of like a Salvador Dali painting. Arriving back at the cemetery, we hopped out of the cab and walked over to pay the guy, but he zoomed-off in a heartbeat. Ha! Leon must have scared the poop out of him, taking us to the graveyard probably didn't help calm his jumpy nerves. We climbed over the old gate and headed straight back to the dying campfire, where we had our fish and chips. And there was Leon's motorbike, just waiting for action. I saw the spinner sitting all alone too, I suggested to Leon that we take it back to the laundromat, and park it down in the underground cave. Leon agreed, begrudgingly. I'd never driven a car before, but how hard could it be? It didn't look too difficult, plus, the spinner had an automatic transmission, I figured it out pretty quick. We drove west, to Portobello Road, parked the spinner down below and got ready to fly. I thought I did quite well, I only crashed into six parked cars along the way, and six is my lucky number, so I was quite pleased with myself. The spinner has a very funny hooter, it sounds like a herd of tired sheep. When I finally jumped into IRON JOHN's side-car, I saw that Leon was smiling, he must have thought my reckless driving was good value entertainment. I drove like a blind old stunt woman heading to the opticians. Driving at half five am is a good time to be out on the streets. I love Betty's spinner, it's a fun ride. I think it was around six or seven in the morning now. I always had to guess the time, believe it or not, I still had my little shooting-star watch on my wrist, but it stopped working years ago. I could never throw it away though, it was my lucky charm, a hearty connection to my old Dad, I kept it for sentimental reasons, it was pretty scratched up now. Leon revved IRON JOHN with no mercy, picking up speed we flew up into the cold morning sky, and what a beautiful scenic sky it was, it looked spectacular, a perfect fiery amber orange glow, with the beautiful rising sun shining strong, over in the distance. At last we were on our way, heading west, it was time to catch up with the gang. Our journey to Hudson Bay had finally begun, yes! The old suitcase full of purple magic was no longer in Leon's sidecar; it was safely tucked away in the back of the ice cream van. I was happy to stay with Leon. It was awfully loud sitting inside IRON JOHN's sidecar, but I kind of liked it. I pretended I was sitting in the cock-pit of an old Spitfire war plane. Leaving London behind, we were now flying over Reading, we'd be passing over Bristol and Cardiff soon. It was a great feeling flying over the English countryside in the morning sun, huge green fields everywhere, stretching out towards the horizon as far as the eye could see, what a treat, the views directly below were fantastic, lots of sleepy sheep slowly waking up in the morning mist, hundreds of lazy cows grazing and lounging around, lots of rivers and thatch roof farm barns. Flying over the south of Wales I saw a beautiful windmill.

We caught up with the guys just as they were flying over Cork, right down in the south of Ireland. The circus sack swung wildly in the wind, but all the witches were bagged up good, they were going nowhere, all of them were still out cold, sleeping the morning away. Max and Penelope kept a good sharp eye on the funny looking sack.

There was just one question I had in my mind…

What about Roaring Meg?

I wondered, where is the old girl?

And what's she up to?

CHAPTER 23

A PUNCH-UP IN THE SKY

As you have probably come to realise by now, Sasha's masterplan was indeed a very unorthodox operation. Meg's plan, however, was quite simple. She wanted to wipe out the whole gang, brainwash billions of people with fear, and take full control over the whole planet. Can you imagine that? Some crazy sicko having the nerve to try and brainwash the entire human race? I mean, how would they do that? Using the power of television perhaps? Roaring Meg's greedy obsession for power made her overlook one very important detail, she completely underestimated the sheer willpower and determination of our unique tenacious gang. When you have a gang devoting all their strength and intelligence to teamwork, well, there's just no telling what they might do. These guys worked together like a symphony of wonder, a synchronised-unfolding of unbreakable greatness, unique individuals coming together as one. Surely, Meg must have wondered why none of her witch Lieutenants had flown back to the moon, to report on their progress. She had absolutely no idea that every single witch was now being transported over the Atlantic Ocean, in a giant circus sleeping bag, ha! She searched high and low for her troops in Camden, but it turned out to be a complete waste of time. After an unsuccessful search she went straight to Betty's aundromat on Portobello Road, but it was all locked-up, all she found was a laminated letter sellotaped to the glass, on the shops front door, the note said...

"Dear Meg, you're a twisted-sicko-loser, and your pathetic plan won't work, so suck on those apples, you old tart! Love from the gang." No doubt this message filled Meg up with poisonous witch-rage, she was so obsessed about getting her revenge on Sasha. He knew Meg would find us, it was just a matter of time, but strangely enough, this was exactly what Sasha wanted, getting Meg to follow us to Hudson Bay was all part of his genius plan. Speeding away, high up in the sky, I looked out the window and saw Greenland under the patchy clouds below us. This indicated that we had now flown more than half way over the Atlantic Ocean, we were now flying above the Labrador Sea, I didn't see any dogs though, ha-ha. Looking over to the ice cream van, I saw Kelly Ann gazing out the back window, she had a very curious look on her face; her psychic powers were twitching all over her body, her instincts were jabbing away, it was like her heart had received an urgent text message, that quickly bubbled-up to her brain. I believe they call that intuition. She turned to the rest of the gang in the van and shouted at the top of her voice, "ROARING MEG IS CLOSE BY. I CAN FEEL HER PRESENCE. SHE'S COMING TO GET THE WHOLE GANG!" Kelly had a few nervous feelings kicking about. Sasha remained cool and calm, as usual. We stuck close to the ice cream van, flying just behind, while Max and Penelope continued circling around the circus sack below. Looking over to the ice cream van once more, I saw Betty and Kelly waving at me, I thought nothing of it at first, so I just smiled and waved back, but that all suddenly changed when Betty held a scribbly sign up that said,

"LOOK OUT, LOUISE. MEG IS COMING FOR YOU NOW!" I quickly looked into the motorbike's side-view mirror and saw Roaring Meg approaching us, what a Crazy Mama! She was riding on her black surfboard. The looney tune was heading straight for us, flying like a wild raging vulture, she looked really ticked off. She waved one fist in the air while her other fist was firmly wrapped around a half-finished bottle of Jack Daniels, she was just about managing to keep her balance, Meg wasn't able to cast any hard-core spells, the silly old cow was up to her old tricks again – drinking and flying, she was completely smashed off her rocker, absolutely plastered, ripped over the rainbow. Leon's driving had suddenly become quite scatty and erratic. Looking over to my left, I suddenly noticed how the whole of Leon's bumpy face had turned all weird and hairy, he jolted about like a freak, he looked like he was having some kind of wack-attack, maybe he was having a wild sneeze-athon. The old hobo couldn't stop jerking around. Something spooky was going here. Jittering about like a fidgety twit, Leon suddenly bowed his head right down, I think he was shivering now. It all started to make sense when I saw the full moon shining its silver light up in the sky. Yikes, Leon was turning into a werewolf. He suddenly raised his head and bellowed out the most fantastic haunted howl ever! It was great! The intense fear I felt in my tummy was primal, in truth, I was actually quite glad to see Leon's transformation. Roaring Meg was ultra-keen and mega-determined to kill and destroy all of us, but we had a spirited were-wolf in our pack now, this gave us the edge we needed, with a cat like Leon on the front line the odds quickly fell more to our favour, he looked ready to go crackie-lackie-loco!

Meg steamed into us like a wild-eyed-gipsy-ghost-rugby-player, landing on the back of the bike she almost knocked Leon off his seat, instantly smashing the whiskey bottle over his head she proceeded to scratch his face up with her long metallic fingernails, she was ratty and feisty, she tried biting into Leon's neck... but her dirty dentures kept falling out. There was a horrid darkness in her dusky voice, "What have you done with all my witches? You crazy ugly-freak!" Leon had fully turned into a murderous werewolf now, this dangerous dude was brimming with dark passion too, I sensed a great wolfy malice, mixed with a raging 'deep-rooted' desire for revenge. He was proper riled up big time. He hated Meg so much, it was like a crazy switch suddenly flicked on inside Leon's head. This was the perfect opportunity to let rip and go full-throttle on her, but Leon had to honour Sasha's instructions, Sasha wanted Meg to be kept alive, this was a real bummer for Leon. Meg suddenly gripped her old veiny hands around Leon's neck, she gave it her best shot to strangle him to death, squeezing his throat with all her might, but this had practically no effect on Leon, he was too strong, too wild, and way too upset to be worrying about a little bit of pain. With no hesitation at all he sunk his sharp wolf teeth deep into Meg's left arm and proceeded to take the biggest juiciest bite he could manage. His spiky fangs instantly ripped out a nice big chunk of green lumpy witch flesh, Leon spat it out into the sky and quickly went straight back in for another bite.

"Mmmmm... Witch blood. My favourite!" He shouted.

Meg's ruby-red-ragu-blood spilled out from her veins, like thick tomato soup, her black surfboard suddenly came whizzing by, it was hovering alongside the both of them now. Meg was in a lot of pain and suddenly had second thoughts about what she was doing. Leon's crazy wolf-rage was terribly powerful, and extremely offensive. Meg felt the full force of his raw anger, and decided to quickly jump back on her flying surfboard. With her dark red eager eyes she looked up above and got ready to make an attack on the ice cream van, but Leon was having none of that, he jumped on the board with her and constantly punched her face-in like he was Rocky Marciano. This really freaked me out, cos I was now left all alone, sitting inside IRON JOHN'S rusty sidecar with nobody at the flippin wheel. Sweet fuzz nuts! Leon and Meg smashed the hell out of each other on that surfboard, they fought like a couple of wild dogs. I watched them rip into each other, then I slowly fell into a kamikaze nosedive. I had to move fast, but I couldn't open the frickin door. Mayday-Mayday! I was going down. Holy Moly! I kept bashing against the door again and again, but the damn thing wouldn't budge, I was trapped. Max Redwood suddenly swished over and bust the door open in half a second. Yes! What a hero! Thank you Max, you little beauty. I climbed over to the driver's seat and quickly grabbed the handlebars. Penelope Jones flew alongside me now. She didn't touch anything, but she gave me lots of encouragement; it was so windy up there. I had to turn this suicidal nosedive around quick-time. I was falling fast, getting too close to the ocean below. I truly wanted to live, so with all my strength I tried to pull-up, after thirty seconds of pure adrenaline, I slowly levelled things out, I just about managed to re-gain some balance, it was such a close shave, let me tell you. IRON JOHN skimmed over the ocean, the tyres kissed the sea surface a few times, then I flew back up into the sky, phew-wee. How close was that? Let's do it again! Ha-ha!

That was my daily dosage of danger done and dusted. Max and Penelope stayed with me after that. Learning to fly IRON JOHN that quick was insane, a very intense crash course indeed, scary but lots of fun. I looked up high and saw that Leon and Meg were still at it, bashing each other's heads in, fighting their hearts out. I looked higher and saw the whole gang come shooting out of the ice cream van. They all flew down to help Leon; it was a spectacular sight to see, everyone had their own jet-powered rocket board. Sasha, Kelly Ann, Tigerlips, Betty, and three of the Fuzzies. Betty stashed lots of spare rocket-boards inside the van, on our last laundromat visit, a savvy move by the pink-headed legend. Fuzz Cat George stayed on board of course, the van wasn't going to fly itself was it. Knowing Betty, she'll probably install an automatic pilot when the ice cream van gets an upgrade. Gliding through the cold sky, the whole gang steamed into Meg, they quickly tied her up with rope and flew her back up to the van. Meg was completely out-numbered. Teamwork baby! Back inside the van they tied her firmly to the passenger seat, she barked and snapped-away like a wild crazy mongrel freak. Leon was so pumped up, full of anger and adrenaline. He wanted to carry on fighting; he wanted to rip Meg apart, take her head off, but he somehow managed to control his wolf-rage, he decided to hang back for a while, he started chewing on Meg's black surfboard, to kill some time.

It was best to leave him alone for the next five or ten minutes, he would have probably killed anyone who approached him, friend or foe, Leon was locked into his wild hunting werewolf mode. The full moon had a very strong effect on this wild winter warrior. Back in the van, The Fuzz Cats quickly teamed-up to give Meg a soul-smacking-hurricane-wacking-ass-whipping-triple-powered-hug-zap. But it had no effect on her; this crazy old mama was too damn strong. They tried ten more zaps, but it was all in vain - the Hug-Zap-formula only tickled Meg. Sasha stepped-up next, he zapped Meg with a mighty-fierce paralysis spell, and she suddenly found herself stuck inside a large frozen block of ice, for a moment she looked defeated, but it only lasted for ten seconds. Meg melted the ice with two fiery laser beams that came shooting from her eyes. Sasha tried another spell, he zapped Meg's body with a huge cloud of purple mist, and when the smoke cleared, she was tied up in a big bundle of thick rope, the same kind of fat rope they use to moor ships, down at the docks. Using the same evil eye-ball laser beams, Meg quickly turned all the thick ropes into flames. Sweet heavens above, this ancient witch was becoming a real jinx of a problem. Betty stepped-up next, she suddenly went nuts, she punched Meg in the face for five minutes flat, Meg just smiled and laughed like a deranged hyena, it was Kelly's turn to have a go now, she quickly pointed her mum's magic wand straight into Meg's ugly boat race. Not really knowing what she was doing, Kelly zapped some untamed magic right into Meg's crimson eyes. This was the first time she ever used the wand, and the spell she threw turned out to be a real corker. Kelly imagined a picture of Meg all locked-up inside a tiny 'solid-steel' cage, and with no hesitation, the magic wand honoured her vision, what a sweet tip-top result. At last, we finally had Meg caged-up and under control. We all kept our fingers crossed now, hoping that the crazy old mongoose wouldn't break free. She was crackers to the bone, apparently she said a great many horrible things to us, her foul mouth was atrocious. I wasn't actually in the van when all this happened, Betty told me everything that went down, a few hours later.

I was still outside cutting through the air, flying solo, I was just about coping with all the pressure. The turbulence and whirly wind pockets pushed IRON JOHN all over the place. Max and Penelope never left my side, they truly are a dynamite pair of genuine buddies. Things were looking good now. We finally had ALL the witches in our possession, and Hudson bay was just up ahead, over in the distance. The biggest ass-kicking wizard spell in all of history was about to commence. I should have filmed it on Leon's iphone, oh well, never mind. Maybe one day they'll turn my life story into a film, wouldn't that be cool.

CHAPTER 24

A TIGERY ACT OF KINDNESS

Cowabunga! We finally arrived at Hudson Bay. It was flippin freezing out in the open air. The cold blue Canadian sky was awfully bitter, but this was nothing compared to what was coming. It was almost time for Sasha's bad-ass spell to work its wonders. Leon continued gliding about on Meg's black surfboard, while I bobbed up and down on his motorbike. His passions were still sky-high, he wanted to rip Meg's face off, literally. I remember how cool he looked standing on her thin black surfboard; his silvery silhouette looked triumphant, he stood all alone with the light of the moon behind him, steam poured out from his mouth when he howled majestically, or was it mist? I don't know. Leon was a pretty good sky-surfer, he had no fear of heights. I'm sure Betty was impressed by his boldness. Trust me, I'm a girl. I looked up to the ice cream van again and saw some movement going on, the driver's door suddenly opened, and Tiger bravely jumped out without a parachute. Like a fearless Tomcat he cut through the sky and swiftly landed on the back of Meg's surfboard, almost knocking his brother off. Tiger quickly wrapped his arms around Leon's waist and ordered his bro to fly down to the bay. Leon did what he was told, but judging by his body language, he probably wanted to give Tiger a good punch on the nose, Leon's blood was hotter than liquid magma.

"Come on! Hurry up, you crazy old wolf. Fly me down lower." Leon wanted to swipe Tiger right across the face for being so bossy, but instead, he did exactly what Tiger instructed. This was 'DISCIPLINED-TEAMWORK-SPIRIT IN-MOTION.' This was a lesson for me, Leon showed me that teamwork is far more important than any stubborn ego can ever be, no matter how strong the individual is.

As they flew lower into the bay, Tiger spontaneously leapt off Meg's board, he dived deep into the ocean performing a 'smooth-double-somersault-flip' before cutting through the surface, what a show-off! He could have been an olympic diver if he wanted to. As soon as Tiger hit the water, he immediately started making lots of weird catty growling sounds, he did this just under the surface. I couldn't figure out what he was doing at first, then Max explained, Tiger was actually sending out warning messages to all the sea-life in the bay. Being one-third stingray and one-third electric eel, Tiger had no trouble communicating with all the sealife in the ocean. He roared ferociously on an ultra-high-aqua-frequency-level, he was basically telling everyone to clear off. "It's evacuation time, so get a move on, and leave the bay area, make it snappy, stay away for at least twenty-four hours," this was the message Tiger roared. Something very heavy was about to go down, I saw the Titanic shipwreck just up ahead. We were so close now. I'm pleased to say that the circus sack was still holding strong - we didn't lose a single witch. The final stages of Sasha's magnificent masterplan were about to kick-off. Yeah baby, this was so much better than having to go to school. Well blow me down, that was a short chapter. This information below has nothing to do with the plot, it's something Sasha once told me about Penelope Jones, it's a pretty cool slice of history, so I thought I'd share it with you. Back when Penelope was the toughest fighter around, nobody, and I mean absolutely no-one could ever beat her. All her illegal boxing matches were carried out on the second floor of an old London pub called 'The Carpenter's Wild Wife.' Penelope reigned supreme, all the local people loved her tough fighting spirit. All the passionate folks and peasants shouting and gambling at ringside called her 'Nell.' "Come on, Nell, knock his teeth out!" She fought men or women, she was ruthless, she'd fight anyone, if the price was right. Then, one day, the local boxing fans started calling her 'Tough-Nell,' and after a few years, her name became legend all over London, and believe it or not, when she passed away, they ended-up naming a train station after her. So, if you ever visit London, make sure you keep an eye out for Tuf-nell Park tube station, on the northern line, this is Penelope's old hunting ground, cool hey, true legends go on and on. Tough-Nell, we still love you, and your ghost big time! x

CHAPTER 25

ONE BAD-ASS WIZARD SPELL

Ok, back to the story, all the Hudson Bay sea-life had now swum out to the North Atlantic Ocean. They heard the warning call from Tigerlips and quickly scooted away.

The ice cream van hovered steady now, about fifty metres above the Titanic shipwreck; this was exactly what Sasha wanted. He grabbed a hold of the steel cage and flew Meg down, on a jet-powered rocket board, Kelly followed on another board, in one hand she held her magic wand, and in the other she held the suitcase full of purple magic. The Titanic shipwreck was barely visible, all of it remained underwater, apart from one of the big chimney funnels peek-a-booing above sea level. Flying alongside Kelly, Sasha gently took the magic wand off his daughter and started using it to raise the Titanic shipwreck up to the surface, this allowed them to land on deck, there were lots of mini icebergs drifting around. What happened next was extremely crazy – this was easily by far the best spell of all time, a very strange and mystical magic to witness, this is the way real magic should be. Well, I half agree, sometimes magic should be as simple as love. As soon as he landed on deck Sasha pointed the wand straight up to the sky, he got busy casting his last spell ever. Now, I know this sounds like I'm talking bananas, but I'm only telling you exactly what I saw, OK. I swear! Pinky swear!

Right off the bat, Sasha's fantastic bombastic spell was bold and blazing, the wand attracted and manipulated vast amounts of rainfall and thunderstorms from all over the world. Sasha skilfully held all the electric thunder and lightning up there in the sky, just above Hudson Bay. The wild crackles of angry lightning and huge rumbles of deep thunder probably made the heavens shake, and the rain came down like crazy. Sasha added another component to the mix now - he coaxed all the Northern Lights from Alaska and Norway, they looked utterly gorgeous, for some reason they call these lights the Aurora Borealis; a mixture of beautiful green-pink-purple lights dancing graciously in the cold, dark wintry skies - they are so damn pretty! Well, Sasha sucked all these Northern lights over to the skies above Hudson Bay as well.

Sasha's spell was colossal, probably the biggest spell ever conducted by a wizard. Fire and ice mixed with electric sparks came blasting out from the tip of the wand, quickly rushing up to the sky, this BOLD MAGIC speedily shaped all the wild untamed weather into a huge green electric horseshoe, this was insane, I had to fly right out of Sasha's way. Mr Sonic looked like he was in a trance, as he entwined all these pure weathery elements together, he used sheer wizardry skill. The huge bright horseshoe lit all the sky up, it was absolutely stunning, it looked like the spell was working, but Sasha still had lots to do. His concentration was deep and serious; things were heating up now. In all honesty, I still didn't have a clue what he was up to. He waved his arms about like a crazy conductor in front of a large orchestra, he suddenly threw the wand up in the air, and caught it with his other hand, ahhhh, he was really showing off now. I suddenly noticed how the Titanic shipwreck began to wobble and shake, that was the moment Sasha looked up to the ice cream van, he gave his signal to the gang. It was time for Betty and The Fuzz Cats to do their part, their job was to release all the green yukky witches. They slowly climbed down the tight ropes of the circus sack and waited for Sasha to give them the green-light-go-ahead. Now flying a little lower, Fuzz Cat George skilfully positioned the circus sack to hover just one and a half meters above the Titanic. Pointing his free hand to the big sack, Sasha nodded passionately to Betty and the three fuzzies – it was time to get busy offloading the green cargo. They carefully opened the huge sack at the bottom and delicately poured the mini-witches out onto the open deck, no sharp sudden moves were allowed. Kelly helped out too. They worked thoughtfully and compassionately, slow gentle handling was the order of the day, they used this soft approach till the circus sack was completely empty. We now had every single witch resting on deck, a huge fat humongous pile of green bony bodies, all of them were still snoozing the morning away, thank goodness for that. Betty, Kelly and the three Fuzz Cats stayed close to Sasha now, they were positively affected by the spells abundant aura, and mesmerised by Sasha's handling skills. The cool wizard quickly refocused all his attention back up to the green electric horseshoe above. I couldn't understand what he was doing, but I knew I could trust him. This ma-hoo-sive horseshoe shined like bright emerald green diamonds; it was the exact same shade as Betty's pretty eyes. Sparks jumped off it, it snapped and popped with pure electric power, then it suddenly began to rapidly expand, stretching right out across the whole bay. The Fuzz Cats loved all the electricity in the air, it made their faces light-up like glow-worms. Leon enjoyed watching Sasha do his thing, still standing on Meg's black flying surfboard he waited patiently for his brother. Tiger suddenly popped his head up from the ocean, Leon glided back down to pick him up. He hopped back on Meg's board with a smile, he was shining bright too like a cosmic fire-fly. Both the Paradox Twins quickly cut through the sky, flying wide to avoid colliding into the green crackling horseshoe, they soon reached the Titanic and safely landed on deck. The horseshoe was colossal now, it grew bigger than Hudson Bay. The next part of Sasha's fantastic spell was to get the Titanic shipwreck into the exact-correct-position, this required great manoeuvring skills. Kelly suddenly noticed that some of the witches were beginning to wake up. No! She soon told Sasha, and he quickly blasted a bright flash of magic over to the pile, they all fell straight back into their springtime slumber, youser! Our supersonic gang leader started lowering the huge green horseshoe down into position, he lowered it to the point where it dipped into the sea, what on earth was he doing? I was still flying about on Leon's motorbike, with Penelope in the sidecar, and Max holding on tight to my shoulder, we all agreed to fly down to the Titanic. The whole gang were together now, apart from Fuzz Cat George, he was still at the wheel of the ice cream van, hovering calmly above us. I looked over to the huge pile of witches and saw that some of them were waking up again, oh pants! They were like those flippin birthday candles that 'flame-up' every time you blow them out... For crying out loud!

Suddenly, right out of the blue, Sasha started barking lots of bossy orders at us, it was difficult to fully understand his words, over the wild sound of the hard-falling-rain, and the electro-static-crackling-horseshoe, it whipped and snapped away like crazy, plus, the awesome magic blasting out from the wand was ever so loud, almost deafening. Sasha shouted over to Kelly Ann, "Kelly, my love, I need you to open the suitcase now, we've got to make sure all the purple magic is in position – please hurry up, my little darling." Making sure it was left wide open, Kelly positioned the battered old suitcase right beside the humongous pile of witches. None of us realised this at the time, but the whole shipwreck was now floating above sea level. It rose out of the ocean and proceeded to climb higher.

"Ok, guys!" said Sasha.

"You must get away from here now, we have a powerful visitor coming to help us, and you need to be at least one mile away, if you want to stay alive that is." Everyone looked a bit confused; nobody knew what Sasha was up to. A visitor? Who was coming to visit us? Santa Claus?

"Come on! Go! Go! Go! There's no time to explain! Get yourselves out of here, NOW!" Sasha shouted like a crazy American wrestler, jacked up on steroids, his voice suddenly cracked, he became all teary and emotional. "Kelly Ann, Betty, I love you two angels with all my heart, but you must go now. Please get away from here!"

Penelope Jones suddenly spoke up.

"Hey guys, do you know what, I think now would be a great time to get a quick group photo."

"Yes, let's do that." Betty had already taken her selfie stick out, why was she so calm? Sasha was under so much stress. This huge spell was all about timing, Mr Sonic had to make sure that everything was ready, and in position… for when the visitor came. The mysterious visitor was bold, cool and beautiful. And she won't be staying long, that was for sure, she was coming soon. Sasha shouted out once again, "Oh my days! Listen guys, if you're gonna take a group picture, will you please hurry up and get on with it. Make it snappy, OK!" Sweet pumpkin seeds, Sasha was so emotional. We all quickly gathered around him, as he held the wand up to the sky, the huge stream of magic blasting out from the old wand looked like a blazing bright craggy moonbeam. We all smiled as we huddled and cuddled up. Something quite funny happened in that moment y'know. I've got the picture in my phone, right in the corner of the shot, I can see Roaring Meg peering out from her steel cage, and it looks like she's trying to crack a little smile. Maybe deep down inside she wanted to be in our gang? Oh I say, more highly classified intel about this will unfold in book two. As soon as the photo was taken, my purple rib picked up a strong feeling of 'Goodbye' in the air, everything suddenly became very serious and adult-like. Strong emotions filled our bodies. I turned around to see Betty and Kelly giving their dad a big hug goodbye, poor girls, they'd spent such little time with him, and now it looked as though he was buggering-off somewhere else. The clock was ticking away, Sasha now used the wand to release Meg from the steel cage, he quickly grabbed and locked her under his left arm, while his right hand continued conducting the mighty fierce electric spell above. Following Sasha's orders, we all scarpered far away from the shipwreck. Betty and Kelly both flew up to the ice cream van on a jet-powered-rocket-ironing-board each, I flew off on Meg's black surfboard; Penelope and Max flew alone. The three Fuzz Cats quickly climbed back up the circus ropes, and Leon and Tigerlips flew off on IRON JOHN. The only ones left on the Titanic now were Sasha, Meg, and all the sleeping witches.

The 'GLOW' coming from the purple magic, inside the old leather suitcase grew bigger and brighter. Remember, there was a great deal of purple magic brewing up inside the ships steel as well, the whole shipwreck started to glow up. Everything was happening harmoniously, just the way Sasha planned, this spell was all about perfect timing, unique synchronicity. Sasha pointed his wand intensely, aiming higher into the sky, stabbing out with more passion, this gesture enhanced all the magic in the atmosphere, huge jagged bolts of purple lightning came spitting out from the wand. It was beautiful and powerful, and it created an abundance of energy, lingering all around the bay. It was so powerful that it turned the green horseshoe into a purple one, it also made my rib glow under my T shirt, things were looking and cooking good now, this mystic magical storm was in full swing. Sasha was very emotional when he said goodbye to his daughters, this made me ask myself a question…

Will I ever see Sonic Sasha again? Or is this the last goodbye? Yikes! I hopped back into the ice cream van with the two cosmic sisters and immediately helped the three Fuzz Cats climb in, Max and Penelope flew in through the driver-door-sliding-window. It was crazy windy up there. Then I suddenly got distracted, something on the dashboard caught my eye, it was an old red shoebox filled with sunglasses for snowboarders, and a small note from Sasha that said: 'PUT THESE SHADES ON. QUICKLY NOW!' We did what were told, and quickly created some distance between us and the Titanic. There was another scribbly message on the dashboard that said… 'ICE LOLLIES AVAILABLE FOR EVERYONE, TAKE A PEEK INSIDE THE SMALL FRIDGE-FREEZER, UNDER THE GLOVE COMPARTMENT. ENJOY! LOVE FROM SASHA.' I looked inside and found seven 'Fab' ice lollies, yummy, nice one Sasha.

The empty circus sack dangled thirty-odd meters below us now, we had to stick to our promise and return it back to the traveling gipsy-circus people in Regents Park, but not just yet – we were in the middle of something unique, and I didn't want to miss a thing. Looking out the side window, I saw Leon and Tigerlips hovering close by. None of us had a clue what was coming next, only Sasha knew. He was a very secretive wizard, I think he enjoyed keeping us guessing, he was very good at keeping us on our toes. We were now in a safe p lace, far away enough to watch the completion of this fantastic-once-in-a-lifetime-spell. Sasha dibble-dabbled the wand in his right hand like he was writing out some 'stream-of-consciousness' poetry on an invisible blackboard; this motion made the massive electrical horseshoe dip deeper into the ocean. All the electrical energy bubbled and fizzed, powerful currents swirled about everywhere. It was a good thing Tigerlips ordered the sea-life to swim away - they would have been electrocuted for sure, frizzle-fried down to their bones, just like poor old Mungo, the stupid witch-cat, R.I.P.

The Titanic shipwreck lifted itself even higher now, creating just enough space for the beautiful electric horseshoe to slide under it's belly. At first, the Titanic nearly toppled over, but it soon locked itself into a perfectly set position. It was now sitting comfortably at the very bottom of this ridiculously ma-hoo-sive purple horseshoe; this was indeed a very rare sight to heed.

Roaring Meg suddenly started to grapple with her old nemesis. I guess she still wanted to kill Sasha, but that was impossible now. He was too empowered by all the magical energy oozing out from the wand and horseshoe. Nothing could stop him now. Sasha suddenly made a very loud noise that sounded like a huge lion's roar. At the top of his voice, he spontaneously shouted out two words: "WAKE UP!" His voice sounded like an electric robot, it echoed all around the bay.

This actually happened a fair distance away, but it still made me jump right out of my skin, Sasha's voice had a primal-alpha-vibration to it, it jolted my tummy and made all the hairs on my arms stand on end, like ultra-thin pins. Every single witch woke up at the exact same time, well goodness gracious me. We all still had our cool snowboarding shades on. Safety first. The whole gang watched and wondered about what might happen next? Then, very unexpectedly, Sasha threw the wand out from behind him, and like an ultra thin runaway boomerang, it spun wildly across the bay, it looked like it was heading straight for The Paradox Twins. Leon raised his right arm and swiftly snatched it out of the sky, he immediately placed it inside his black leather jacket, and that's where it stayed, for safe keeping. His wild wolf passion was finally calming down. We all turned our heads back to the Titanic after that, and that's when we saw Sasha hugging Meg with all the wizard love he could muster. We immediately noticed how every single witch had become hysterical with rage, they were all steaming into Sasha, expressing a fierce desire to kill him. It was hard to see every detail, cos we were so far away, it looked like a riot was kicking off. For a fleeting moment our hearts got soaked with sadness, it looked like Sasha was about to meet his demise, but deep in Sasha's heart, none of this really mattered, he didn't give a damn. All t hat mattered to him was staying close to Meg, and all the mini-witches; the biggest surprise was still yet to come. Sasha wouldn't let Meg go, that was for sure, he had a good firm grip on the old girl. I suddenly heard Max whistle a melancholic tune, he was feeling so sad, poor little Max, things were suddenly getting heavy for us, awkward feelings stirred about inside all of us. Looking out over yonder, I saw a big green bundle of bodies moving about, with Sasha and Meg squashed deep underneath. I think I saw Sasha's foot sticking out, I wasn't sure, I needed a pair of binoculars to be honest, Sasha had big stinky feet, but I couldn't smell them now. I smelt something, I think someone in the van let one go, it was Fuzz Cat Sam, he released an electric sparkle bum popper! Ha! It was hard to keep focus on all the witchy activity, we had our own problems with the wild weather. The horseshoe, what with all its bold magic, created a powerful whip-swirl, it blew us all over the place. Fuzz Cat George did his best to fly straight and steady, he was a good pilot. The rioting witches made horrible noises, yes there was a great distance between us but I still heard their high-pitched bitching and moaning; they whined like old pussycats yearning for milk. It was an ugly sound, and a ghastly sight to see. The pile of stinkin' witches grew higher and higher, Sasha and Meg were completely out of sight now, buried deep under all the rioting witch bodies. Here's a quick poem I wrote....

"An ugly green mountain, made from morbid witches, makes me wanna go... dig some more ditches, bury the witches deep in the ditches, slap their face, smack their bottom, bury their bones deep, till their rotten and forgotten." Poetry helps me sometimes. Looking out over Hudson Bay one more time, I saw some interesting movement come from the old brown leather suitcase - the purple magic had suddenly come to life. Yes! It moved about like a small blobby ghost, I watched this tiny cloud of purple mist re-position itself right in the middle of the big pile of rioting witches. What the hell was going on over there? I would never have guessed what was going to happen next, I just watched-on with vivid curiosity, I took another bite out of my 'fab' ice lolly. I wish those fab lollies had more chocolate on them, they're my second favourite ice lolly in the world, give me a 'Nobbly-Bobbly' any day. Suddenly, all the serious heavy magic in the sky changed from weird to wonderful, it became lighter and more tender, and much brighter too. Oh I say, maybe this was Sasha's visitor/friend arriving? Far away in the distance, right at the top of the sky, I saw something approaching the bay. I had no idea what it was, but it seemed to be something that possessed an extremely powerful light. As it got closer, I watched the horseshoe grow bigger. Everything was ready, all in position. It was a good thing I had my sunglasses on, the brightness was insane.

Traveling faster than a speeding bullet, I saw an unidentified object come flying down towards us.

"Look!" shouted Betty.

"It's Halley's Comet!"

WOW!

It shot straight past us!

Oh my goodness, I was awestruck. I watched Halley's Comet come flying down into the bay like a glittery bomb; it moved so fast! It rushed down towards the Titanic, and automatically slotted itself into one side of the huge purple horseshoe. Let me tell you exactly what happened…

IT SWOOPED INTO THE HORSESHOE, SWISHED DOWN TO THE BOTTOM, ZIPPED AROUND… AND QUICKLY CAME BLASTING OUT THE OTHER SIDE.

RACING BACK UP INTO THE STARRY SKIES IN TWO SECONDS FLAT!

AND IT TOOK ABSOLUTELY EVERYTHING WITH IT! EVERYTHING!

Halley's Comet took Sonic Sasha, Roaring Meg, all the mini-witches, the old Titanic shipwreck, and ALL the purple magic, straight back up to the stars. EVERYTHING got catapulted into space by hallelujah Halley. This was the fastest U-turn in history, and the coolest rescue ever.

At the exact same time of the rescue, Sasha instructed all the purple magic to turn Meg and the witches (along with himself) back into shooting stars. Halley's Comet simply gave them the big 'kick-start' they needed. But this time, just by sheer chance, Meg, Sasha, and all the mini witches melded into one big shooting star. They looked like a space rocket shooting up to the top of the sky – a big silver firework destined to race and shine across the universe forever. Halley's comet veered off to the left while they swished off to the right. We all watched with our mouths wide open; thank goodness we had our dark glasses on, Max had a tiny pair of shades too, Sasha thought of everything. We all gazed-on and marvelled at the amazing sight before us, it was astonishing, we were speechless. Just below us, Leon and Tiger watched the spectacular transformation as well. They protected their eyes with tinted motorcycle goggles.

All of us were very impressed with the grand finale of Sasha's one-of-a-kind masterplan; it was a huge success, what a strange unorthodox hero Sasha turned out to be. Maybe he's an Aquarius? He sure did talk a lot. That was the last time we ever saw Sasha, or Meg. It turned out to be a very triumphant day: this was the day two old shooting stars got turned back into one brand new supersonic shooting fire-rock. Sonic Sasha and Roaring Meg finally made it back home, all done with a little bit of help from Halley's Comet. They were flying high, right at the top of the sky, when POOF! They suddenly disappeared, after that the horseshoe disappeared, and all the thunder and lightning and rain began to drift back-off to other parts of the world, all the Northern Lights drifted away too, fat clouds parted, and we suddenly found ourselves sitting in the middle of a beautiful blue sky morning. Penelope Jones spoke up,

"Well, I must say, that was the second best thing I have ever seen in my life."

"Really?" I asked.

"I'm curious, Penelope… If Sasha's unique spell came in second place, what, in your opinion, is the coolest thing you've ever seen?" Penelope smiled,

"Rocky One, of course. It's a no-brainer. I absolutely love a good boxing movie." Penelope was loopy, all the way down to her bones, but I loved her so much, I'd actually grown to love every single member of this gang. All of us were still affected by the remaining wind pockets and shreds of invisible magic, lingering all over the bay, I guess we needed to find a way to calm our nerves.

We soon decided to land in a nearby Canadian forest, we set the van down in a place called Wapusk National Park. Everyone was overwhelmed with high emotion mixed with a feeling of loss, as more minutes passed, things starting to level out, a slow 'comedown' kicked-in, and that truly was the toughest part of our day.
We needed to relax and chill, just for a half hour or so.

We soon found a barbecue area with numerous fire-pits and solid wooden picnic benches, we decided to start up a camp fire and boil up some water, we made green tea and cooked some marshmallows on a stick.

Why not?

This little time-out helped us wind-down and slowly get centred again.

It wasn't easy calming down after all the wild stuff we'd been through, on a personal level, I was still busy processing everything, saying goodbye to Sasha was the hardest-highest-hurdle to get over.
I kept having to remind myself that, even though our captain was gone, he was still alive and happy somewhere else, and looking at the whole gang, I kept reminding myself that I was still in tip-top excellent company.
I just hate goodbyes. They really suck!

CHAPTER 26

THE EXPLODING DIAMOND EXPRESS

He'd only just left us about twenty minutes ago, but all of us were already missing Sasha like crazy. It made me feel good inside, knowing that this cosmic sky wizard finally got back up to where he belonged, and it was terrific to know that Meg had left all her dark evil ways behind her. Deep down inside this made all the gang happy, but our leader was gone, and that hurt! Sasha was many things to us, a great father figure, our captain, our inspiration. A sinking feeling of grief ran through the whole gang, it felt like we were at a flippin funeral. Betty and Kelly cried their hearts out, many tears raced up their foreheads, vanishing into their lovely hair, I was crying too. The Fuzz Cats and The Paradox Twins looked pretty sombre. Max Redwood sang the blues on my shoulder while Penelope sobbed on Leon's motorbike, she was in a right state, weeping like a broken-hearted little girl. She loves Sasha so much! We all do. Nobody had a clue about his bizarre and mystifying lucky horseshoe; he kept all the details of the supersonic Titanic spell to himself. It made me smile knowing he was free again, but we all missed him terribly, and we never got to say goodbye properly, everything happened so quick. I guess this cosmic experience was just a part of living in the everyday realms of weird worldly whimsical wizardly ways. Hello. My mood suddenly changed, my heart lightened-up, it was like I found a little bit of sunshine waking up inside. This positive wave got triggered off by a tickling sensation in my rib, it stirred about under my t-shirt; it does that sometimes. Sasha's rib was tugging and poking at me like an impatient kid, it told me about a letter in Betty's back pocket. I hesitated for a moment, then I gently asked Betty to go ahead and check her bum pockets, her beautiful green eyes were drenched with tears, bless her, she dipped her hand in her back pocket and slowly pulled out a perfectly folded piece of paper, she quickly opened it. "It's a letter from Dad," a new smile graced her face, the whole gang suddenly perked-up a bit.

"Ok, listen up guys, I'm going to read it out."

We all waited, with a new feeling of excitement in our hearts. Betty coughed, then she began,

"Dear Gang,

Hi guys, Sonic Sasha here. I just wanted to express my gratitude and congratulations, I want to let you guys know that I love you all, so very much! I'm so proud of you. You all came together and worked fantastically well, like a magnificent dream-team. Holy smoke, you guys are the best! Thank you so much for your commitment to our cause and mission. I feel so honoured to have been a part of this uber-cool gang. I've got all of you here with me, deep in my heart, now and forever. And for the record... I want you all to know that I would love to fly down and but as you have probably already guessed, I'm not a wizard anymore, I've gone back to being a shooting star, which means I won't be able to just pop down and say hi, I'm too big and powerful for stuff like that. I've got to stay up here now, in space, this is where I belong, space is my home. Constantly zooming around is the way I roll baby. I need to let you guys know that the heart visit we shared inside Max has created an unbreakable connection between all of us, it's something we can all feel, a sacred bond, we are a solid pack now. I may be millions of miles away, but I still feel all the feelings you guys feel – your joy, your happiness, your sadness, I feel all of it. When you're all feeling good, I shine just that little bit stronger, I fly and race faster, I become a more magnificent shooting star. The same thing goes for ANYONE reading these words, when someone chooses to FEEL GOOD on planet earth, it helps make all the stars shine stronger. Einstein knew all about this, when you break everything down, you'll soon discover that we're all just star-dust, and I want EVERYONE TO SHINE STRONG, this is real love, it's what we're here for. So please do your best while you're alive my friends, try and stay positive down there on planet earth. It's a beautiful lovely planet, just keep the TV switched off, and remember to make jokes and have fun, laugh, dance and giggle. I mean this from my heart, guys! Don't hold on to grudges or resentments, let em go. You don't want to end up like Roaring Meg do you? Keeping tons of anger in your heart is pure poison, it's an awful way to exist. Screw that! You guys need to rise above all that stuff - you must never forget this. You can always float above anger, fear and dark energy. Just follow your heart, it's not pathetic or corny, it's choosing to be wise. I want to give my Italian coffee bar to The Paradox Twins, I think you guys will be happy there. Just try not to scare all the customers away, tell them you like dressing up for Halloween all year round, and make sure you look after Max, give him birdseed and fresh bread every day please. As far as I'm concerned, this tenacious gang still exists, you guys are still a strong unit. Ok, so, I'm not in the gang anymore, but that's no reason to break-up. Look at AC-DC, they carried on when Bon Scott died, and they did alright. I want you guys to promise me that you won't waste your lives watching rubbish TV, and spending too much time on your phone. Don't waste time playing computer games, read Lord of the Rings instead, or learn to play a musical instrument, learn to enjoy life. Spread love, listen to The Beatles. Don't let yourselves become brainwashed by dark energy and all the low vibrations created by the greedy twits out there. Meg forgot who she was, she lost track of her real self. She was angry, lonely, full of dark intentions. I say screw the darkness, focus on the light, and just keep movin forward. Hooooo-Yeeaaah! Meg's long-term plan was to brainwash people, make them feel sad and depressed. She became a twisted control-freak, but that's all over now. She's up here with me, riding shotgun, I know space travel will keep her happy. I want all you guys to be a good example of how fantastic it is to be a little bit weird, a little bit different. Always be true to yourself, be who you really are. It's cool to be a little bit kooky and eccentric - embrace it. Cock-a-doodle-doo! I want to tell Kelly and Betty that I'm so proud of the both of you. I love you girls, so so much! Your mother, Jennie the mermaid, has gone back to the ocean, but I must implore you to go find her, I'm sure Tigerlips can help. I want the both of you to try and reconnect with her, really get to know her, she wants to see you guys again - she loves you so much, it's been too long. My DNA is very strong, this is the main reason why you two girls never developed any mermaid fins, or gills. You took after me more than you took after your mother, but there is one thing you all have in common - you're all gorgeous and beautiful. I want to tell you about my other rib now. I left it deep in the soil, back at Highgate Cemetery. It's a gift for Jennie. It has intelligent magical energy inside it, just like Louise's rib. It's patiently waiting to make Jennie happy again. This rib will let your mum transform herself into a woman any time she likes. She can be a mermaid or a woman, it's up to her. I think I still love her, holy smoke! Ha-ha! My darling Betty, please know this, you can find my second magical rib in the exact same spot you found Louise's rib, it's buried six foot deeper, all Jennie has to do is wear the rib around her neck at bedtime, and when she wakes up the following the morning, the rib will be inside her. I would like you guys to give Jennie's wand back to her as well, I hope one day she'll help Kelly Ann understand its true powers. This wand has many deep beautiful secrets. Leon will look after it for the time being.

I also want to express my hearty thanks to The Fuzz Cats. You guys rock! You're the coolest electric cats in the universe. Thanks for all your hard work and unbreakable commitment."

Betty took a break from reading the letter. There was more to read, but we all needed a little timeout, to digest everything Sasha said. Still perched on my shoulder, Max Redwood started to sing a sweet happy melody. That was a good sign, he immediately took advice from Sasha's letter, Max became more cheerful in a matter of seconds. I really liked having Max on my shoulder, it made me feel good inside knowing that he chose to be close to me before anyone else in the gang; he was a cool robin. Betty was now ready to continue with the letter. Sasha was talking to me now.

"I now have something to say to Louise Buttersky: I need to apologise for all the trouble I've put her through. I think Louise has been a brave little member of this gang. She's had a very rough time with the way things went for her, and it's high-time she knows the truth about her folks. I was there when they disappeared on that sunny afternoon, in the hot air balloon. I was the guy on the beach, dishing out the balloon rides for twenty quid; that was me in disguise. I was the one who took your parents away Louise. I'm so sorry about this, honey, but I had to do it; I needed to protect them. I'm sorry for putting you through all that tough stuff, Lou-Bee-Lou. I know you've missed your parents dearly, but I did this because I knew just how crazy Meg was. She would have killed your Mum and Dad, without batting an eyelid. Meg was consumed with greed, anger, rage and selfishness. She knew nothing about kindness; she simply wanted to control everything, and reign supreme. She would've happily murdered your parents, just to get to you. That's when I boldly decided to intervene and take your folks away, keep them out of Meg's reach y'know. Louise, you'll be very pleased to know that both your parents are alive and well, out in Hawaii, I set them up in a fantastic little business, they run a cool little restaurant on Ewa beach, in Honolulu – it's called the BAMBOO BOOGIE BURGER BAR, and they're expecting you. They want you and the whole gang to drop in for burgers and milkshakes." My O My! We all looked at each other with excited eyes; ZING! My heart suddenly felt like singing. Yeeeeeee-Haaaaaaa! And Yippee I-A! I asked Betty to read that part of the letter again, just to make sure I heard what I thought I heard. She read it out, and I began to cry. Holy smoking flip flops! I was going to see my parents again, thank god for that! A warm feeling of love suddenly filled my body, it was like my heart suddenly turned into a boiling hot water bottle, I was overwhelmed with waves of happy feelings.

Youser-Youser-Youser! Tigerlips spoke up. "That all sounds wicked man, I could murder a juicy Hawaiian burger with sweet potato fries on the side, wash it down with a thick cold strawberry shake, this green tea sucks!"

"Yeh, I fancy a burger too, a nice bloody rare one," said Leon.

Sasha's fantastic letter cheered everyone up. I suddenly felt happy, scared, excited, and nervous all at the same time – it was great. I couldn't believe it. I was going to see my Mum and Dad again, wow! What a day!

"Is that the end of the letter?" I asked.

Betty looked down and said,

"No-no, there's a little bit more." This is what it said:

"Now listen guys, I want all of you to get back in the ice cream van, and Leon, you get back on your motorbike. I want all of you to promise me that you'll go straight to Honolulu and have a big party in my honour. Get your funky asses over to the Bamboo Boogie Burger Bar, let your hair down, wet your whistles, and have some good old-fashioned fun. Do that for me please, cos I love you all. I want you guys to celebrate your magnificent achievements. Together we have gotten rid of Meg and all the mini witches, but more importantly, we've gotten rid of Meg's dark morbid twisted will, and that's a huge achievement my friends, a perfectly valid reason to have a great swinging party.

Always remember guys, that:

TEAMWORK MAKES THE DREAMWORK!

Now, get going!"

As soon as Betty finished reading the letter, she raised her head and smiled, and everyone cheered out loud. We all felt so much better after hearing Sasha's wise, caring words.

Penelope suddenly spoke up,

"Come on guys, let's go. Everybody back in the ice cream van, hurry, hurry!" We were all so excited. The Fuzz Cats glowed up like Christmas tree lights, my heart was overwhelmed with joy. We all climbed back inside the van, while stubborn Leon hopped back on his triumph motorbike. He made a quick announcement, just before we took off. He said he was happy to take the circus sack back to the travelling gypsies in Regent's Park. We all thanked him, and helped tie the big tent to the back of his motorbike. Penelope decided to go with Leon; she loved sitting inside IRON JOHN'S rusty little sidecar, she said it was cosy, she's a sweet old ghost. They swiftly flew off, heading straight for London, while the rest of the gang flew to Honolulu.

The Fuzz Cats behaved like perfectly well mannered waiters up in the air, acting like happy-go-lucky-jolly-trolly-dollies, they served drinks for everyone, and with a little bit of soft ukulele strumming, they sung several more songs for all of us to enjoy, my personal favourite was an old number called,

'PAPERBACK WRITER,' by The Beatles,

What a great song!

Pure mustard.

I think I was the first kid ever to hear...

'The Fuzz Cats-Ukulele Version,' ha-ha.

About twenty minutes before we arrived in sunny Honolulu, me and the gang got into a nice conversation about Sasha and Meg's new shooting star.

Because the star was completely brand new, we all decided to give it a brand new name,

We called it...

'The Exploding Diamond Express.'

It left Hudson Bay like a first class dynamite speed-racer.

Nice one Sasha!

Just want you to know that....

The whole gang loves you too x

CHAPTER 27

ALOHA

Arriving in hot sunny Honolulu was like stepping into a postcard, blue skies and sunshine all along the way. Fuzz Cat George landed the ice cream van on the flat sands of Ewa beach, the wind from the spinning majestic Titanic propeller upset all the local sunbathing tourists, beach towels, bikini-tops, and loose garments blew all over the place, ha-ha. Sorry about that. I was so excited! I felt so good inside; I really thought my parents were dead. Betty felt my joy as she held my hand, she was like a big sister now, I always wanted a sister. Betty was kind of surreal y'know, yet deeply authentic, in fact, that comment goes for the whole gang. Looking over yonder, I saw a fantastic palm tree with two beach shops positioned down by its trunk, the first store was a typical ocean shop, they had wet-suits, T-shirts, sun lotions, sunglasses, surfboards, stuff like that y'know. The place next door had a cool wooden sign that said, 'The Bamboo Boogie Burger Bar,' yeh baby, the search was over, the eagle has landed, ha-ha!

"Come on, let's go grab a burger," said Tigerlips. Everyone, apart from myself, felt hungry. I couldn't think about food; I had too many emotions dancing around inside my little body. I had busy butterflies in my heart, happy thoughts in my head, and jumping jitterbugs in my tummy. I already felt full up. No room for food, well, maybe later. We got some strange looks from all the sun tanned tourists on the beach. You don't see creatures like The Fuzz Cats and Tigerlips too often. Kelly and Betty looked pretty bing-bong too. I probably looked like a little looney tune, what with my blue hair and a cosmic robin perched on my shoulder, but I didn't care, I was happy. It's so important to remember to never give a damn about what other people think. Max kept busy singing beautiful lovely music, quick happy melodies came blasting straight out from his little heart. I guess Leon and Penelope were probably in London by now. It was awfully nice of them to return the circus sack. They'd join us soon enough, no doubt about it. We were now standing outside the main entrance of The Bamboo Boogie Burger Bar, everyone suddenly stared down at me, not a word was spoken but all eyes said the same thing, I should go in first. So, I took a deep breath, slowly walked in, and immediately saw both my parents at the bar. Mum was cleaning the coffee machine while Dad mopped the floor, they had a small silver digital radio playing Hawaiian music in the background, it was playing my favourite song ever, a track called, 'Somewhere Over the Rainbow,' by a big chubby Hawaiian guy called Brother IZ. I bet he had over a hundred Bamboo cheese burgers back in his glory days.

"Louise, is that you? Oh my goodness!" Shouted my Dad. My heart swiftly flickered, as it skipped a couple of beats.

"Louise! My lovely Louise!" Dad dropped his mop and ran straight over, swooping me off the ground like a big loving grizzly bear he hugged and squeezed me with all his heart. We spun around and around; I felt like the richest girl in the universe. He cried like a big baby, and so did I.

My mum screamed and cried-out with uncontrollable joy,

"Louise! My sweet Louise!"

She hopped over the bar and immediately put her foot in the metal mopping up bucket, mama tripped over and fell flat on her face - ha-ha, oh my goodness, she was so excited. She quickly bounced back up and ran over, throwing both her arms over me and Dad. We were a happy family again, at last! Yes! The gang were sobbing too. My goodness, I had so much to tell them. I introduced Mum and Dad to all the guys. Everyone was so pleased to meet my parents; it was a lovely occasion. Hugs all round.

"I'll have one of your finest Bamboo Burgers please, Sir," said Tigerlips to my dad. "Yes, of course," he said, while hugging Tigerlips. "Bamboo Burgers for everyone. And thank you so much guys, for looking after my daughter." As soon as all the introductions were finished, Dad went to the kitchen and cooked up a storm of treats, Mum made over a dozen yummy milkshakes, and a strong black Brazilian coffee for Betty, that beautiful zany laundromat lady sure loves her coffee. Mum made her shakes with a big industrial blender, she threw dollops of vanilla ice cream in with lots of chocolate coated foam banana sweets. Everyone raised their milkshake glasses up high, we all made a toast for Sasha. When we finished our burgers and shakes, a man wearing a cool Hawaiian shirt came walking into the restaurant, he briefly spoke to my mum. He was a native, a laid back delivery guy called Ernie, he had something special for us waiting in the back of his truck, the item he was delivering was nothing short of pretty damn fantastic.

Scratching his head, Ernie checked out the whole gang with a spooked expression on his face, he slowly walked back out to his van, and soon came back with a huge American jukebox, he rolled it in on a big old trolley; it looked so cool. It was a classic Rock 'n' Roll vintage Wurlitzer. Ernie placed it in the corner of the restaurant, just by the little checkered dance floor. The Fuzz Cats helped move it into position; they were good at removal work. This jukebox played real vinyl records for 25 cents a song. It was so cool. What a beauty. It had a big red bow tied over it, with a little note attached to the side that said, "Hey guys, it's time for all of you to dance your blues away. Keep smiling and party on, love from Sasha x." That was all it said, so without wasting a second, we plugged it in and played lots of great music for hours and hours on end - party time had arrived.

The Bamboo Boogie Burger Bar was the right place to be, if you liked dancing your ass off, and Dad's burgers were so tasty. Like crazy fools we danced to great fifties and sixties music as the sun went down. Then we danced some more.

I guess it was around nine thirty when Leon and Penelope arrived. In no time at all, Leon filled his belly with burgers, hot-dogs and milkshakes, and soon after that he was flipping through all the jukebox songs, looking for his favourite Johnny Cash track, 'Folsom Prison Blues.' Leon and Penelope soon joined in with all the celebrations. We were a far cry away from all the stolid stubborn individuals gathered around Sasha's dining table, back in Italy, back in chapter fifteen. We were loosy-goosy now, bouncing around like happy kids. I think I saw some angels dancing with us too, it was cool.

I was laughing so hard at the way Leon danced; he was a lovely character when he opened-up. The Fuzz Cats had some funny moves too, they were breakdancing. Tiger and Kelly were inseparable, they danced together for hours. Betty was having a lot of fun dancing with The Fuzz Cats, she did the Tango with Fuzz Cat Sam, she looked over at Leon many times, but he didn't know how to make his move. Max stayed on my shoulder the whole night long, he was my new best friend. There was a happy silly song on the jukebox called 'Bamboo.' It was very stupid and really funny, it made us laugh constantly, so we played it over and over. We also played 'Kiss' by Prince, and 'Starman' by David Bowie, a tribute to Sasha. Penelope danced on the bar like a drunk, happy monkey, and Leon danced with my mum, he was moving and grooving like John Travolta from 'Saturday Night Fever.' We were all having a magnificent time. The loud music filled the bar and spilled out the doors and windows, the happy Bamboo vibes enticed lots of passing tourists and local folks to come inside and join the groove. More people kept arriving, as the music played throughout the night. This was the happiest day of my life. I was reunited with my Mum and Dad, and I now had a whole new bunch of fantastic friends: the magnificent tenacious gang, they felt more like family to be honest, I was truly blessed to be in such magnificent company.

Fuzz Cat George suddenly came up to me, he had a little gift in his hand. He was holding the original lullaby music box from the flying ice cream van.

"Here you go, Louise, this music box here is a small gift from The Fuzz Cats. It's our calling card, it plays a song called YOU'LL NEVER WALK ALONE, just hit the switch and we'll come running straight to your aid, and if that doesn't work, just send us a text message. Ha-ha." George was sweet, he gave me a high-five, did a cartwheel and quickly acted out some crazy dance moves, he wiggled his bum as he waltzed back over to the dance floor; he made me chuckle. It was a lovely gift. I needed to take a break from all the euphoria, all this good stuff going on left me feeling quite overwhelmed, I decided to go outside for a breather, I needed some fresh air. I walked out onto the beach and took many deep breaths, the gentle salty breeze of the cool night air soothed the skin on my face, it felt lovely. I looked out over the ocean and saw the last tip of the setting sun slowly disappear. See ya tomorrow sun x

Dad was all set-up on the beach with a big barbecue now, he cooked for everyone.

"Free Burgers. Free Kebabs. Come and get it folks." He was busy for hours. Kicking my shoes off, I decided to walk further out along the sand, I strolled down the soft beach for quite a while. I needed to digest everything in my heart and soul. All this good stuff was quite a shock to my system y' know, a nice shock, but still a shock nonetheless. Walking barefoot on the beach felt divine, I looked up to the sky and saw the North star gracefully shining down on little old me. I had so much to be grateful for. I felt so happy to be alive.

I suddenly felt a deep powerful warmth come up from inside me; it was my rib, glowing up again. It felt so positive and strong. I turned and looked to Max on my left shoulder, he immediately whistled a few happy notes, then I suddenly noticed something up in the sky.

It was Sonic Sasha and Roaring Meg passing by on the Exploding Diamond Express. I couldn't help myself – I started to cry.

I had so much love for Sasha.

Like a mesmerised kid at Disneyland I reached out to touch him, silly I know. It didn't take long for them to swish over the Hawaiian Islands, they left a sparkly message in their trail, written in bright shiny stardust, the message said…

"KEEP SHINING, LOUISE!"

I smiled and blew a kiss up to them, holy minestrone, I suddenly felt my tears run up my forehead, instead of down my cheeks, another cool gift from Sasha's magic rib. Drying my eyes I calmly walked back to the Bamboo Boogie Burger Bar, and spent the whole night dancing with my friends and family. Max never left my shoulder the whole night long, in fact, he's still here with me now, doing a crossword, while I'm typing these words into my lap top.

As more time went by, I got fed up with having to constantly repeat myself, explaining my adventures to new friends and other folks, so I decided to put my story into a book, a book that you've just finished reading.

Thank you so much for joining me on this crazy adventure.

Until the next time, this is Louise Buttersky saying goodbye and ...

KEEP SHINING!

Hi, this is Tony Andrews.
Thank you so much for reading
'Louise Buttersky'

Take Care, Stay Positive,
Go After Your Dreams,
Keep Cool,
and
KEEP SHINING!

Louise Buttersky will return.
(Book two coming soon)
(Louise Jade Buttersky)

For more information please visit ...
www.tonyandrewsmusic.com

Thanks!

Bye for now.
from
Tony Andrews

Check out Tony's second book,
7 Wacky Tales, eccentric short stories
for everyone! (8+)

www.tonyandrewsmusic.com